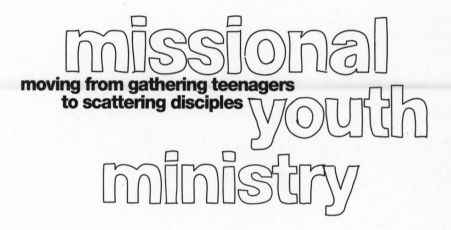

missional youth ministry

moving from gathering teenagers to scattering disciples

missional youth

moving from gathering teenagers to scattering disciples

youth ministry

brian kirk & jacob thorne

youth specialties

ZONDERVAN.com/
AUTHORTRACKER
follow your favorite authors

ZONDERVAN

Missional Youth Ministry
Copyright © 2011 by Brian Kirk and Jacob Thorne

YS Youth Specialties is a trademark of YOUTHWORKS!, INCORPORATED and is registered with the United States Patent and Trademark Office.

This title is also available as a Zondervan ebook. Visit www.zondervan.com/ebooks.

Requests for information should be addressed to:

Zondervan, *Grand Rapids, Michigan 49530*

Library of Congress Cataloging-in-Publication Data

Kirk, Brian.
    Missional youth ministry : moving from gathering teenagers to scattering disciples / Brian Kirk and Jacob Thorne.
      p.   cm.
    ISBN 978-0-310-57884-0 (softcover)
    1. Church work with youth. 2. Discipling (Christianity) I. Thorne, Jacob. II. Title.
  BV4447.K565 2011
  259'.23 — dc22   2010043579

Cover design: Mark Novelli, Imago Design
Interior design: David Conn

Printed in the United States of America

12 13 14 15 16 17 18 19 /DCI/ 20 19 18 17 16 15 14 13 12 11 10 9 8 7 6 5 4 3

This book is dedicated to all of the youth we have had the privilege to serve with in ministry. Each of you helped make this book a reality

contents

acknowledgments

The completion of this book would not have been possible without the many acts of help, encouragement, and support we have received along the way. We owe a huge debt of gratitude to everyone at Youth Specialties for taking a risk on two new writers. We especially wish to thank Jay Howver for the first breakfast meeting and believing in us; Roni Meek for all of her support along the way; and our amazing editor, Carla Barnhill, for challenging us, pushing us, and helping us create a book that became more than we had envisioned.

We also want to thank Eden Theological Seminary in St. Louis, Missouri, and the dynamic professors who encouraged us during our time as students to learn how to reflect theologically, think critically, and challenge others to seek a deeper and more meaningful life of faith in Christ.

introduction

Not long ago I (Brian) told Jacob about my first fall as a youth minister. It was more than 20 years ago now, and at the time it seemed like every youth ministry book suggested that a good youth leader should know just the right combination of games, themed events, road trips, and parties to keep the youth active and interested in church. In addition, a good youth leader should kick off the school year with a big, splashy event that was designed to bring back the old group and hook a new bunch of kids. This event should show teenagers that church can be fun and exciting and wacky! I was new, untested, and eager to please. And my new church had placed a great deal of trust in my ability to develop a thriving youth ministry. So if the books said it took exciting programming to draw teenagers, then we'd have some exciting programming!

That fall our opening event was a beach party in the church parking lot, complete with a huge pile of sand (deposited by a local construction company). A big crowd of teenagers attended—wearing their Hawaiian shirts, of course—and they really seemed to enjoy the food, the water balloon fights, other water games, and the chance to make sand castles.

There was just one problem: By the end of the event, I wasn't sure the youth had any idea they were at a church or even participating in a Christian ministry.

And, to top it all off, in all of my grand scheming and preparing, I'd forgotten to make a plan to get rid of all that sand. The solution? Let's just say it involved a shovel, a wheelbarrow, and many, many hours of my time. Thank goodness I had the back of a 23 year old.

Twenty years and several churches later, things have changed dramatically. Last fall as I prepared to begin another new year of ministry, there were no plans for an event large enough to attract half the teens in town. The ministry team wasn't worried about kicking off a school year full of high-energy and entertainment-fueled activities. Instead, we opened the evening with a quiet prayer, a meal, and a time of sharing our summer experiences with one another. It was a warm evening, so then we headed out to the side yard of the church to put our artistic skills to use creating tie-dye shirts and fabric squares.

The shirts were for the teenagers to wear as a way to develop a sense of connection with the other people in the group. The fabric squares were for a group art project. Each person attached his or her square to the others to create a quilt. We then invited the teenagers to reflect on the symbolism of this multicolored creation, patched together from unique works of art created by each member of the group.

Never let it be said that young people cannot verbalize their understanding of community, grace, forgiveness, peace, love, and the movement of the Spirit. The quilt was the perfect catalyst for giving youth a way to talk about their understanding of Christian community, where each person is loved and accepted for his or her uniqueness. We continued to add squares to the quilt as new friends joined the group throughout the year. And that quilt still hangs in the youth room today to serve as a reminder to always make room for others in the circle of the Christian family.

The contrast between the beach party experience from 20 years ago and the more recent quilt project is significant. One focused on entertainment and distraction, while the other focused on creativity, community, worship, and contemplative reflection on what it means to be children of God in relationship with one another. The beach party kicked off a year of activities that, by necessity, had to get bigger and better just to keep the teens coming. The art project and worship service created a pattern for a ministry year characterized by the creation of authentic Christian community. When I look back on those two Septembers, I realize that—in some small way—they represent the points along the journey of many youth ministers who've stopped and said to themselves, *There must be a different way.*

For decades so much of youth ministry has been program-driven—serving teenagers with the assumption that its primary function is to use activities and events to attract young people to church and then keep them occupied until they're ready to be adult members in the faith. However, in recent years it's become increasingly obvious that this paradigm has failed to help teenagers become lifelong participants in the Christian church and the Christian faith.

Recent research by the Barna Group reveals that 61 percent of people in their 20s who were active in a church during their teens are now disengaged from active participation in worshipping communities and spiritual activities, including prayer and Bible study. The research also concludes that the old assumption that young adults return to church when they become parents is no longer a given. Many will stay disengaged even into their 30s.[1]

A 2007 study by LifeWay Research (the research arm of the Southern Baptist Convention) found that 70 percent of the young adults they studied left the church after age 18, with only 35 percent returning to regular participation later in their 20s.[2]

Perhaps most notably, a 2010 study by the Pew Research Center found that only one-third of people under age 30 attend worship services regularly, and less than half consider religion to be important to their lives.[3] It

---

1. Barna Group, "Most Twentysomethings Put Christianity on the Shelf Following Spiritually Active Teen Years," September 11, 2006. http://www.barna.org/barna-update/article/16-teensnext-gen/147-most-twentysomethings-put-christianity-on-the-shelf-following-spiritually-active-teen-years.

2. LifeWay Research Staff, "LifeWay Research Uncovers Reasons 18 to 22 Year Olds Drop Out of Church," http://www.lifeway.com/article/165949/.

3. Allison Pond, Gregory Smith, and Scott Clement, "Religion Among the Millennials: Less Religiously Active Than Older Americans, But Fairly Traditional In Other Ways," The Pew Forum on Religion and Public Life, February 17, 2010. http://pewforum.org/Age/Religion-Among-the-Millennials.aspx.

isn't that these young adults aren't spiritual, the report concludes. Rather, they don't find the kind of spiritual experiences they're seeking in churches.

This research has profound implications for youth ministry. The teenage years are a prime time to engage youth in the real, missional activities of the wider church, engaging them in a faith that's meaningful and makes a difference in the world. Instead, most teenagers' primary church experience is a series of segregated activities, most of which bear little resemblance to the practices of the rest of the church. Consequently when teenagers graduate from high school and youth group, they feel like their most meaningful church experiences have ended. In short, the program-driven model of youth ministry has failed to help young people find their place in the church.

Our goal in *Missional Youth Ministry* is to offer more than just a critique of this older paradigm. We invite you to rethink many of the deepest assumptions of youth ministry. This book serves as a theological companion and practical guide for all those who are working in the trenches of youth ministry and seeking to offer teenagers a deeper, more mission-oriented, and lifelong relationship with God. We want to take you beyond planning events and organizing games to a place where you can help teenagers develop the kind of faith that will matter to them today, tomorrow, and for the rest of their lives.

In the following chapters, we challenge the consumerist goal of judging a ministry's success by the number of participants. We push back against the notion that a youth ministry can be summed up by the events on the calendar. We reconsider the place of volunteers and parents, calling for adults to see themselves as more than chaperones. We send out a call for greater understanding of the current approaches to teaching and the impact of educational theory on the intellectual and spiritual development of teenagers. And we project new models of worship that will help teenagers see these elements of the Christian faith not as isolated activities, but as the very heart of our journey with God.

Back in 2006, we began this conversation on our blog, Rethinking Youth Ministry, because we believed there must be other youth workers out there who were struggling with the same questions.[4] We're grateful for

4. www.rethinkingyouthministry.com

the many youth workers in the blogosphere who joined us in our *rethinking* and our search for a deeper, more thoughtful approach to youth ministry by responding to our weekly blog posts with their own thoughts and questions.

In this book we share some of our original blog posts, each representing the struggles, challenges, and dreams of two ministers in the thick of youth ministry. These posts served as a way to jump-start our journey of rethinking and reimagining a new way for the future. As you'll see, we've deepened our thinking on many of these original posts because of the interaction with the wonderful men and women who were willing to share their experiences and expertise with us in the public forum of a blog.

We hope our journey will inspire you to develop a missional youth ministry. If you're feeling stuck or burned out or unmotivated, we want to lead you into a more fulfilling model of ministry. If you've sensed the need for change but haven't known where to start, we want to help you embrace new ways of offering teenagers the life-changing ministry you always hoped was possible. If you feel like you're in competition with every other church in town, we want to free you up to create a ministry that's meaningful for you and your teens. And if you find that your teenagers are falling away from the church once they graduate, we want to give you permission to leave behind the consumer models of ministry and move toward an approach that's centered in the radical and life-giving way of Christ.

We wrote this book as partners. In the first two chapters, we speak with one voice as we lay the foundation for missional youth ministry. Beginning in chapter 3, we engage in more of a conversation, with one of us writing each of the remaining chapters. (You'll see a name at the beginning of each chapter to let you know who's doing the talking.) Then at the end of each chapter, you'll find a response from the other author. We hope this back-and-forth, dialogical approach creates a model for all of us who love youth ministry—one in which we share our best ideas with each other while still pushing one another to stronger, more meaningful engagement with teenagers.

chapter 1

rethinking youth ministry

Where did we ever get the idea that successful youth ministry was about numbers? If that's really the case, then we might be two of the worst youth pastors in the world. Some of the youth ministry programs we've served actually got smaller during our tenures. Oh, we had a good number of teenagers in attendance when we took road trips to amusement parks or carpooled to the bowling alley. But if you counted heads on the Sunday nights devoted to a discussion of Christ's radical call on our lives, you wouldn't find much of a crowd.

Even when we leaders are comfortable with a small, meaningful experience, we all worry that someone *is* counting heads every time our youth groups gather. We know there's a line of thinking that says growth is very much the point of youth ministry. And there are people who will remind us that we can offer deeply moving worship nights, the best Bible studies, and the most amazing mission trips; but it doesn't make any difference if the church across the street is attracting more teenagers.

Original Blog Date: December 21

It's ridiculous how many times in recent memory I've been with folks connected to youth ministry and someone has said, "You need to check out what so-and-so is doing. He's got over 100 youth in his program," or "She is doing some great stuff in youth ministry. You should see the tons of kids that are participating." . . . Stop equating success in ministry with how many people you can attract. Stop confusing consumer culture with the mission of the church. Scripture depicts Jesus as focusing most of his time and teaching on just **twelve** people! I think there's a lesson in there somewhere. —Brian

It's Not about Numbers

Back in the '50s and '60s, the church I serve in urban St. Louis welcomed hundreds of children and teens to Sunday school every week. Now they have an average attendance of 15 young people and children on a Sunday morning—the result of urban flight and changing cultural values.

Sometimes (only sometimes) it seems life was easier when we were kids. Families ate dinner together every night, kids could roam their neighborhoods without fear of strangers, and Sundays were church days. When I was a kid in Jefferson City, Missouri, they still had the *blue laws* that meant almost every commercial business was closed on Sundays. You could still buy groceries (not beer!), but there were no shopping malls, bookstores, bowling alleys, or movie theaters enticing us away from home, family, and church. As children we hated this kind of stuff. But as adults, we tend to look back on those times with definite nostalgia for something lost.

Now it's a whole new world. Teenagers miss morning worship—sometimes for weeks on end—because of sporting events and practices. They miss church and youth group because of school play rehearsals, weekend jobs, and Scouting activities. There is so much to do that a course called "Enticing Teens to Come to Youth Group" should be taught in seminary. Such a class could prepare youth ministers for the phrase we dread hearing on Sunday mornings: "What are we doing at youth group this week?" This question always comes from the mouth of a young person who was raised and baptized in the waters of a consumerist culture that provides endless options for how to spend our time and resources. If we come up with a less-than-enticing answer, we can almost guarantee we won't see that kid at youth group that week.

Youth leaders are often reluctant to say anything about these inevitable scheduling conflicts. We resist even making the suggestion—to youth or their parents—that church and worship and youth group can't make the kind of impact they might when a teenager is there only every other week or whenever there isn't something else going on during that time. Because church is voluntary, we don't believe it's our place to demand a higher level of participation and fidelity to the church body. And, unless you serve in a megachurch, maybe you're just a little afraid that if you push too hard, the teenagers will stop coming altogether. So you ease off for fear of sending the youth group into a downward spiral.

We've both felt this fear a few times—the I-don't-want-to-get-fired fear. Somehow we become convinced that no matter what other good we might accomplish, our success in youth ministry has everything to do with how many teenagers walk in the door on Sunday or Wednesday nights. Yet it's this sort of fear that stifles ministry and keeps us from introducing teens to a truly radical faith that has the power to transform lives.

Original Blog Date: August 8

This past Sunday I had the opportunity to preach on the Markan passages related to the feeding of the 5,000 and Jesus walking on water—an interesting challenge for someone who reads much of the Bible as metaphor. My sermon primarily focused on the walking on water story and the Markan theme of fear. In the passage the disciples see Jesus coming across the water, but they don't recognize him. They think they are seeing a ghost and freak out! Of course, in Mark's Gospel, the disciples are always having trouble understanding who Jesus is—they just don't get him. At the end of the Gospel, their fear wins out over their trust and they run off to hide.

My time in youth ministry has taught me that many of us who minister to young people are constantly operating under this sort of "fear factor." We're often paralyzed in our effort to offer an authentic faith experience to our youth because we fear that if we do, (1) it'll bore the teens and our group won't grow and, consequently, (2) the kids will stop coming and the group will shrink, (3) the church won't think we're successful in terms of numbers and activity, (4) everyone will find out that we don't exactly have this youth ministry thing down to a science, and (5) we will fail. —Brian

So we play it safe. We stick to our comfort zones and to the comfort zones of our youth—movie nights, pizza parties, Christian concerts, and trips to amusement parks—when what teens really need is quiet, rest, time alone with God, authentic relationship, and a chance to see the reality that exists just beyond the veil of our consumer culture.

The challenge for those of us in youth ministry is to get beyond our fears and anxieties and trust that God is already working in the lives of these young people. Our task, perhaps, is simply to provide quiet spaces where they can hear God's call on their hearts.

It's Not about Entertainment

For both of us, there have been defining moments that changed our perspective on youth ministry. For me (Brian), it was a weekend youth retreat.

It was one of those beautiful end-of-summer Missouri weeks when the weather was perfect. My small youth group of mostly girls and a few gangly boys loaded into three cars and journeyed to Camp Walter Scott for a weekend getaway. We'd picked this time of year on purpose. It was a chance for the teens to enjoy the last moments of summer without the distraction of homework and school activities that were just a few weeks away. We came for the swimming, the hiking, the canoeing, and the campfires. Most of all we came to steal a few moments of rest and silence and fellowship with friends.

The weekend was over too soon, and as we gathered together for our final early morning worship, several of the youth stepped forward to lead the service.

Original Blog Date: August 30

The setting was an outdoor chapel that looked out over the campground's lake. Communion elements were grapes and a loaf of bread. Two girls in our group shared the words of institution from Scripture and then invited the others forward. With big smiles on their faces, they received each person and offered them the symbolic elements of Christ's life and ministry. I took my place in line, received the elements, and sat down. Then I noticed that some of the youth had returned to the line for a second helping! Imagine that: wanting to receive a double portion of Communion. One of the other adults looked at me as if to say, "Is this okay?" to which I replied, "Hey, we need all the Communion we can get!" As more people got back in line, the ritual of Communion took on a festive atmosphere as we were indeed sharing in a real meal together. The typical staid atmosphere of the Communion service turned festive with the youth talking and laughing with one another. —Brian

I remember wondering at that moment, *Why can't worship, why can't church, why can't youth ministry be like this all the time?* Here, in the simple beauty of nature and the sharing of a few morsels of bread and grapes, we felt enveloped in the amazing abundance of the kingdom of God. Was it possible that in this moment our teenagers were experiencing joy, true community, and perhaps a glimpse of God's vision of the world where all have enough, all are fed, and all know they are cared for and loved? Was it possible that this kingdom moment came without the setting of a state-of-the-art youth building, video game systems, Christian rock music, projected imagery, wild games, and a crowd of fellow teenagers? Could youth ministry really happen without all of the trappings that our culture tells us are so important if we want to attract teens to the church?

That weekend was a reminder that sometimes the simplest experiences in youth ministry leave the most lasting impressions. It was also a reminder that they happen only when we stop worrying so much about how others may judge our ministry, get out of the way, and leave space for God to be present.

One of the most amazing results of letting go of our fears and trusting God is that we discover youth ministry isn't all about us. We discover that it isn't about how charismatic we are, or how many teenagers we attract to the ministry, or how competent we are at developing great programming. As we let go of our anxiety about numbers and stop focusing on what our ministries look like from the outside, we're free to allow the Spirit room to move inside our ministries. We're free to remember that the Spirit—not our programs—will draw young people closer to the heart of God.

We're also free to stop churning out activities for the sake of having a full calendar. In so doing we make space to ask a more important question: *Why have a youth ministry program at all?* With all the energy we expend trying to attract youth to our churches with flashy and entertainment-centered programming, perhaps we've forgotten to ask why we want all of these teenagers there in the first place. More importantly, perhaps we've failed to offer our young people a strong, compelling reason to be at church beyond the lock-ins and weekend retreats. What do we say if they ask us, *"Why come to worship? Why be a Christian? What difference does it make?"*

So What Is It About?

The pressure to create big programs that pull in big numbers isn't necessarily about greed or competition. At many churches there is deep concern for the eternal salvation of teenagers. There is a real desire for teens to be *saved*. When that's the primary concern of a ministry, the numbers *do* matter—the more souls saved, the better. But following the way of Christ means more than focusing solely on the life to come. We have only to look to the Bible to know this is true. The bulk of the Gospel texts go into great detail about the way Jesus lived, the way he loved, the way he reached out to others and served those in need. These stories inspired the members of the early church to call themselves Followers of the Way long before the term *Christian* was in use.

It is this way of being in the world, this way of living and loving, this missional kind of faith that we're called to guide teenagers toward. This ministry perspective can be life changing, but it also can be challenging. It's not always popular and, for some young people, it might seem less attractive than the entertainment-fueled and consumption-centered culture of their everyday lives.

If youth ministry isn't about making teens into Christians (that's the work of the Holy Spirit, after all) and it's not about the numbers, then what is the purpose of youth ministry? We've wrestled with that question many times. We're convinced it's time to lay a new foundation for youth ministry that goes beyond the promises of eternal life and the focus on numbers, and toward a lived faith that's centered in the way of Christ.

chapter 2

the foundations of missional youth ministry

About a year ago, we asked the question *Why youth ministry?* on our blog. We posted our thoughts and asked our blog readers to contribute their ideas as well. After receiving input from youth leaders from all kinds of churches and in all kinds of places, we indentified seven foundational goals upon which to build a rich, meaningful, and theologically sound missional ministry with youth.

Youth ministry should:

1. Introduce Teenagers to the Christian Faith

So often we assume that young people who've grown up in the church know the basics of faith by the time they're 15 years old. They've been to Sunday school, so they know all about Noah's ark and the Ten Commandments and the parables of Jesus. What's left to teach them? Aren't they ready to go out into the world and evangelize others into the faith? The short answer is *no.*

Mike Yaconelli, the cofounder of Youth Specialties and an inspiration to untold numbers of youth workers, believed that teens are too young to be disciples. He said,

Young people are too . . . well . . . young to be disciples.

Apprentices? Of course. Beginners? Sure. Trainees? Interns? Absolutely. But not disciples.

We've convinced adults and parents that we have programs that can produce disciples. We perpetuate the illusion that we can take 13-year-olds and make disciples out of them. We actually act as though we can transform a group of inconsistent, uncommitted adolescents into mature, committed disciples by spending an extra hour or two a week with them.

Not possible.

Are students capable of heroic acts? Absolutely! Can a 13-year-old be committed to Jesus? Yes . . . as long as we understand what we mean by "committed." Can young people make a difference in the world? Of course they can, but we're still not talking about disciples.[1]

We believe that becoming a disciple of Christ is more than a statement of belief. Becoming a disciple means taking a journey. It means developing a heart for missions and service to others. It demands thoughtful and regular study of Scripture. It requires a willingness to sacrifice, to walk through some of life's fires, and to wrestle with the deep questions of faith. Many young people have yet to give themselves over to this commitment. Youth ministry is meant to introduce teenagers to Christ's radical, boundary-breaking way of peace and justice and to help them figure out what it means to follow him. It's a place for them to be Christians in training.

It's crossed our minds more than once that youth leaders are not so much nurturing the teens in our groups right now as we are nurturing who they might be when they're 21 or 25 or 30. Much of what we do in youth ministry bears fruit years later, perhaps in ways we'll never know. What we're teaching them now may not really connect with them until they're older and have more experience with the challenges of life. It might

---

1. The Yaconelli Family, *Getting Fired for the Glory of God: The Collected Words of Mike Yaconelli* (Grand Rapids, Mich.: Youth Specialties/Zondervan, 2008), 116–117.

not mean much to them until some piece of Scripture, some experience in missions, some compassionate moment offered to them in their teens helps them be the person they were created to be.

On the flip side of this reminder is one of the dangers of youth ministry: Neither you nor your teenagers know what sort of influence you're having on them. So be careful what you say and do—you never know when they're paying attention. Even when you think your actions and words are beyond reproach, be mindful that the teenage brain is still a work in progress. We don't know how our young people are processing what we're teaching them. It's important that we strive to do more than just pour our own dogma, beliefs, and interpretations into their heads. We can't assume they'll simply absorb our worldview and our spiritual mindset.

Original Blog Date: November 7

I was talking with Josh, one of the talented and devoted adult leaders of our youth program. It was shortly after seeing the documentary *Jesus Camp*, and I was commenting that one thing that distinguishes fundamentalist evangelical teens from teens we see in our mainline church is that the evangelical youth really know what they believe. Those Jesus-Camp kids can tell you exactly what they think about God, sin, the afterlife, salvation, etc. Our youth, on the other hand, probably couldn't articulate any definite thinking on those subjects. Josh's response: **"I'm not sure a teenager *should* be able to give you a definite answer about those things."** Though a part of me wants to provide youth with a basic set of Christian fundamentals, a greater part of me agrees with Josh. Teenagers don't necessarily need answers about faith. Rather, they need to be shown how to ask lots and lots of questions. And, just as importantly, they need a safe space in which to ask them. —Brian

Helping teenagers grow stronger in the Christian faith goes far beyond having them memorize Scripture or learn Bible stories or creeds. Young people need the tools to look at Scripture and church teachings critically. They need the freedom to ask questions and challenge assumptions.

They also need us to show them all the ways they can seek God. We need to help them experience the truths of the gospel through a variety of means—including, but not limited to, art, music, poetry, film, service to others, Scripture study, theater, nature, solitude, silence, and prayer. Our goal should be to help teenagers interact with the gospel in such a way that they take ownership of their faith journeys.

In chapter 7 we'll consider more specific ways of developing a thoughtful educational plan and approach to teaching and learning in youth ministry.

2. Enable Youth to Build Community

At its very essence, the Christian faith is about community. It's built upon an understanding that we're in relationship with a God who recognizes that all individuals are worthy of love. Youth ministry should help teenagers learn what it means to live in a radically open and loving community that reflects God's love for the world. Youth ministry should offer opportunities for teenagers to experiment with what this sort of community might look like. It should provide a glimpse of what it means to be loved unconditionally. It should help young people work at loving others—even when it's difficult.

A few years ago I (Brian) had an interesting conversation with a guy from my youth group. This student was about to graduate and wanted to talk with me about some challenges he was having at home. As we talked he mentioned something that had happened recently at youth group that hurt him deeply. During a time of sharing, he'd told the group that his parents' marriage was falling apart. But after he finished speaking, no one said anything. He felt like his revelation had landed like an invisible bomb in the room as we moved right on to the next person. Perhaps the most troubling part for this young man was the fact that he knew other kids in the room had similar situations at home, but no one was willing to talk about it.

It's not easy to create an atmosphere where people will be real. And adults aren't necessarily any better at it. At some churches there can be an unspoken understanding that people shouldn't bring their hardest struggles out in the open or say anything that others might not agree with. I once served with a senior pastor who told me there were two things he never discussed at church—politics and religion—because both topics just started arguments.

So much of our time at church is spent trying to be polite and to appear as though we're the *good people*, the *whole people*, the ones who have our acts together. Our young people pick up on that attitude and believe that's what the Christian life is supposed to look like—either you don't have any problems or you do a good job of keeping them to yourself. Teenagers need us to show them that we all have problems and that Christians should be more keenly aware of the troubles of the world and of daily life. They need to know that church is a safe space to really talk about the hard times of life, about the issues and concerns we all struggle with every day.

Our youth programs need to be more than just places where kids come and have fun and laugh and play. They need to be spaces where teenagers can genuinely express their deepest questions and concerns and know that although we may not have all the answers for them, we will love them and embrace them and walk alongside them.

On the other hand, youth group doesn't have to become a confessional—it's far too easy for times of sharing to become overly dramatic and spiral into an attention-getting contest. But by creating safe communities based in trust and honesty, we can help our young people learn how to come before God and admit their mistakes. We can remind them that they aren't revealing anything God doesn't already know. We can model repentance, forgiveness, grace, and compassion and help our groups do the same. We can help them take a step toward understanding that, despite our mistakes and our sin, we're in relationship with a God who calls us beloved.

In chapter 4 we'll take a more in-depth look at this understanding of community in youth ministry.

3. Guide Teens in Discovering Their Spiritual Gifts

Our young people are bombarded with messages that tell them their self-worth will ultimately be tied to the size of their paychecks and their ability to be good consumers within our capitalist economy. Throughout their adolescence young people are pushed to recognize and hone the skills that they (and their parents) hope will someday make them financially independent.

But what about those gifts that aren't obviously marketable—gifts for discernment, healing, prophecy, mercy, and hospitality? What about the notion of using our gifts to benefit and edify others—not just ourselves? Youth ministry can help teenagers see that they have God-given gifts that cannot be measured in dollars and cents.

Helping young people discern their spiritual gifts and how they might use those gifts in service to God is perhaps one of the most important callings of the youth leader.

Original Blog Date: July 10

Here's a suggested approach for easing your youth into discovering their spiritual gifts:

Have a talent night. I'm serious! The best learning always starts by connecting with something the learner's brain already knows and is comfortable. Encourage your youth group members to come ready to share their talents, gifts, abilities, and interests. Yes, this evening could include the typical singers, actors, and musicians. But also encourage your artists to showcase their works, the poets to give a reading, the athletes to display a trophy or two, the comedians to tell a joke, the juggler to put on a show, the math whiz to solve a quadratic formula, the carpenters to display their handiwork, and so on. Those who don't have a talent that's easily put on display can describe their gifts to the group.

Identify personal spiritual gifts. After the talent show, help youth identify some of the more applicable spiritual gifts they find in Scripture. Together read Romans 12:4–8 and 1 Corinthians 12:1–11, 27–28 and ask what jumps out at them. Prepare a list of spiritual gifts and their descriptions to hand out. You might include such obvious gifts as wisdom, healing, prophecy, service, giving, teaching, and mercy. But I wouldn't limit the list to just the obvious ones enumerated in these passages. Also consider less obvious spiritual gifts such as craftsmanship, music, and writing. After talking through the list, ask the teens to imagine an invisible line going down the center of the room. As you read through the list of spiritual gifts, invite the young people to stand at one end of the line if they think they are strong in a particular gift, at the other end if they think they are weak in that gift, or somewhere in between. Invite them to explain their choices, if they choose.

Identify spiritual gifts in others. This may be the most powerful part of this study. Go through the gifts again, inviting group members to name those people in the group who are particularly strong in each gift. Such an activity helps to illustrate that we often fail to recognize our own gifts until they're recognized by others. Be certain that all teens are lifted up in this process of discernment. If you have a large gathering, you may need to split into smaller groups. Such a naming of gifts can be a real bonding and nurturing experience for a group.

Explore ways to use your gifts. Close with a time of discussion about how God might use any of these particular gifts in ministry. When I've done this activity with a group, the teenagers were pleasantly surprised to consider how the gift of making people laugh could be used in healing or how the gift of prophecy might mean the ability to tell your friends the hard truth even when they don't want to hear it.

How many of us first heard the call to ministry because someone else recognized our gifts long before we ever paid any attention to the Holy Spirit's whisperings? Naming teenagers' spiritual gifts can be a powerful way to affirm their intrinsic worth as children of God, while challenging them to seek ways to use those gifts in doing God's work in the world.

We'll take a deeper look at this approach to missions in chapter 3.

4. Empower Adults to Serve as Spiritual Companions to Young People

Let's face it: Being a teenager is tough. Not many of us would choose to relive those days even if we could. Teens struggle with issues of self-worth, confusion about their identity, and worries about fitting in with their peers.

Therefore, adolescence may not be the best time to force-feed Christian dogma, drill memory verses from Scripture, or expect teens to be able to draw the path of Paul's missionary journeys on a map.

Besides, given the distractions of adolescence, it's unlikely that any of our young people will even remember all of those great Bible studies 20 years from now. But what they *will* remember are the adults God put in their lives—adults who cared enough to put up with their growing pains, listen to their questions, take them on mission trips, and let them stay up all night at the lock-in with their best friends. Youth ministry should offer teenagers the mentorship of faithful adults who will love them just as they are, walk with them on their spiritual journeys, and help them navigate the challenges of adolescence.

A simple way to help create such relationships can be found in small groups. For example, back when we served at the same church, we created small groups out of our Sunday night youth group. Each small group (composed of four or five youth) had an adult sponsor. Sometimes during youth group gatherings, the small groups would meet for more in-depth discussion of the night's teachings. Other times the small groups would meet on a weeknight for pizza, bowling, or some other activity. By spending intentional time with teens outside of our regular youth group meetings, the adults really got to know the teenagers in their groups. It makes such a difference in the lives of young people when they develop relationships with adults who are active in the ministries of the church.

Perhaps one of the greatest challenges of any youth ministry is to find adults who are truly committed to cultivating quality relationships with teenagers. A church that Brian served in years ago really struggled to motivate young people to attend the Sunday morning worship services. As a result this church inadvertently created the dreaded "youth ghetto," in which the teenagers attend Sunday evening youth group but have very little connection to the wider church.

Eventually Brian realized the teenagers weren't the problem. It was the adults. The biggest hurdle to getting the teens more involved in church wasn't the sermon or the style of music. It was convincing the adults to engage in meaningful interactions with the teenagers whenever they were present. When the adults never interact with the teenagers who attend their church, those teens won't rush to come back.

We're not suggesting that young people have no responsibility when it comes to developing relationships with adults in the church. But as adults, we have to recognize that teens are still growing and learning. It's up to us to create a worshipping community that welcomes, includes, and embraces adolescents. It's also up to some adults in the church to do the extra work of fostering meaningful relationships with youth *beyond* the walls of the church.

Ultimately it's the calling of youth workers to be present with youth—listening when they need a friend, attending the important events in their lives, sharing in their joys and troubles, and modeling what a life of faith looks like.

We'll look at the role of adults more closely in chapter 6.

5. Awaken Youth to God's Presence

Many teenagers have lived so long with the idea that God lives *"up there"* or *"out there"* that they find it difficult to figure out where God really is in their lives. Youth ministry can help young people tune in to the God-saturated world we live in by introducing them to a variety of Christian spiritual practices that can awaken their sensitivity to God's presence.

Original Blog Date: October 27

We've been trying to introduce our middle schoolers to the ancient Christian practice of Lectio Divina.[2] The first night we tried it, I was met with some resistance. As soon as I set a pile of Bibles in the middle of the floor, one of the girls, Kelly, announced, "Oh no! Not Bibles! I'm not reading the Bible." (Clearly she'd rather play Duck Duck Goose or talk with her friends.)

Despite Kelly's protests, I went ahead with the meditation on Jesus blessing the children (Luke 18:15-17). The group tolerated

---

2. We'll say more about this practice in chapter 8.

the repetitive readings, the long pauses, and even the silence. But when I asked them to share their reflections on the text, they were (surprise! surprise!) uncharacteristically mute. Nobody wanted to share. I allowed more silence, knowing that someone usually speaks up to fill the dead air. Guess who spoke up first? Yep, it was Kelly—the one who wanted to run from the Bible like a vampire from garlic! Kelly said the part that resonated the most with her was the one about the parents bringing their children to Jesus. She remarked how she wondered if those kids even wanted to be there, being pushed through the crowd and put up in front of everybody, having this strange guy blessing them. I was stunned. That detail of the story had never occurred to me. I'd never thought of it from the children's point of view. (And perhaps Kelly was thinking about how she, and other teens, might feel if forced into a similar situation.)

I then asked them to talk about which character in the story they most related to at this point in their lives: Jesus, the children, the crowd, or the disciples. Again, dead silence. Then Kelly spoke up a second time: "I guess I would be most like Jesus. My mom is going into the hospital this week for surgery, and she wants me to be there with her because she said it will make her feel better. So my being at her bedside will sort of be healing to her. Like Jesus is when he touches the children." Hmmm. And Kelly was the one who didn't want to read the Bible.

Lessons learned: (1) never underestimate your youth, and (2) never underestimate the power of contemplative spiritual practices such as Lectio Divina to open hearts and minds to the truths of our faith. —Brian

The use of spiritual practices in youth ministry can awaken young people to God's call in new ways. These practices can make God's love real for teenagers as they begin to see God in the people and the places of their daily lives. Perhaps most importantly in our fast-paced culture, youth ministry can lead teenagers to be more aware of the ways God's presence can be felt through times of intentional silence and rest.

We'll invite a closer look at ways to rethink worship and prayer with youth in chapter 8.

6. Help Teenagers Discover Sabbath

Each fall, during the second or third week of youth group, Jacob asks the youth in his group to write out their typical Monday schedule from the very beginning to the very end of the day. In the instructions he encourages them to list as many details as possible. And the first time they tried this activity, the results stunned Jacob.

It's not unusual for teenagers to begin their days as early as 5 a.m. In addition most of them sleep with their cell phones either in bed with them or nearby—the texting begins at an early morning hour. Many of them start their day at school, arriving by 6:30 a.m. and putting in a full day of classes and activities. They get home around 6:30 p.m. and try to unwind, eat, and catch up with their social network. Then they start working on their homework before finally heading to bed around midnight.

When Jacob looked at these teenagers' daily schedules, he couldn't believe it. But as he listened to the youth tell their stories, Jacob realized how much pressure—whether real or perceived—that today's teens feel to succeed. He recalls asking the question: *Why do you keep this type of schedule?* This is what one girl wrote in response:

> I work hard and take extra classes in order to get good grades and a good resume so I can go to the college I want. Once I get to college, I'll keep the same schedule and agenda. I need to do well in college so I can get good grades and a good job. I need to get a good job in order that I can make lots of money. I need to make a significant amount of money in order that I can support my family, buy a large house, and take nice vacations. I need to have a good job in order that I can retire well and live comfortably.

Jacob realized his young people needed to take time to slow down and experience the Sabbath that God demonstrates in the very first book of the Bible.

Instead of playing exciting games and activities, try leading your group through experiences that are based on finding rest and balance. Include times of silence during youth retreats. At the end of every youth group meeting, create a quiet atmosphere with prayer and music. On mission trips encourage youth to leave behind their cell phones and disconnect from the daily busyness of life. It's a challenge to get young people to simply slow down and relax. But in order to experience God's presence and God's purpose for their lives, teenagers must learn the spiritual discipline of Sabbath.

7. Help Teens Practice Hospitality and Fellowship

Teenagers are incredibly open to the sacredness of the moment—the realization that God's presence surrounds us on a daily basis. They just need someone to point them in the right direction.

Several years ago Jacob's youth group had the opportunity to serve on a mission trip to New Orleans. On the second day of the trip, one of the work crews went to the home of Harold and Rose. Before the group started working, Harold and Rose wanted to share their Hurricane Katrina story with the volunteers.

Despite the mandatory evacuation orders, Harold had decided to stay home while Rose went to the safety of their children's house several hours away. Harold explained that their life's possessions were in that house and he couldn't stand the idea of leaving. Harold thought he was going to be okay. He watched the television and heard the weatherman say, "It's going to be all right, folks. The worst of the storm has passed." And then, just as the weatherman signed off, the side door of Harold's house caved in, and the water started flooding his house.

For the first night, Harold stayed in his attic, praying the water would recede. The second day he realized he was trapped and had to flee. He made his way through the water to a warehouse where he spent the week waiting to be rescued. A month later, when Harold and Rose finally returned to their home, everything they owned was destroyed. They had little flood insurance, and their homeowner's insurance only covered the roof.

Harold had spent 40 years as a New Orleans police officer. At first glance he's a little intimidating. But as he told his story, tears welled up in his eyes. You could sense the trials and tribulations this man had experienced in the wake of this disaster. Shortly after the storms ended, one of Harold's friends (a fellow police officer) killed himself after learning his family had drowned while he was called in to work during the hurricane. Harold shared how he'd found his own mother dead in her house.

Finally Harold had reached the end of his rope. He was physically and mentally exhausted. He'd lost his faith and had nothing left. Then teams from work camps entered his life and helped him gut his house and start the long process of rebuilding. With a shaky voice, Harold told Jacob's work group, including 10 teenagers, that if they hadn't shown up, he was just days away from going out on the back deck of his house and killing himself—just as his friend had done. But because of the group's hospitality and willingness to serve others, he'd recovered his faith, found strength, and believed he would survive.

That day, that hour, that moment was transformative for the youth group. Through shared hospitality and fellowship while sitting in a driveway in the Lower Ninth Ward, those young people experienced the presence of God. No one returned from that mission trip unchanged.

Hospitality is a central tenet of the Bible. Jesus says, "I was hungry and you gave me something to eat, I was thirsty and you gave me something to drink, I was a stranger and you invited me in" (Matthew 25:35). And in the book of Hebrews, we're reminded: "Do not forget to entertain strangers, for by so doing some people have entertained angels without knowing it" (Hebrews 13:2).

Solid Ground

Your success in achieving these seven foundational goals in your own ministry has nothing to do with how many teenagers your program attracts or how you compare with the church across the street. Your ministry has its unique context, challenges, needs, and gifts. Ultimately, you'll want to discern—through conversations with other adults and the young people in your setting—what and how God is calling you to be.

We believe in the importance of the foundational goals we've listed here, but this list isn't exhaustive. After posting these goals on the blog, our readers added even more. And that's how it *should* be as each of us seeks to develop a ministry that's grounded in Christlike relationships, thoughtful study of Scripture, the nurturing of spiritual gifts, and opportunities for life-changing experiences of worship and missions.

In the chapters to come, we'll unpack each of these elements as we consider our call as adults walking with teenagers on our shared journey of faith.

Rethinking Your Own Ministry

- Consider the foundational goals of youth ministry covered in this chapter. Which of these goals fit your current approach? Which goals challenge you the most? What would you add to the list?

- Evaluate your current or proposed ministry with youth. What are the theological assumptions that drive your ministry?

- How would you respond to the question, *What is the purpose of youth ministry?* Invite other adults and young people to respond to this question and compare their responses to your own. What common assumptions and goals do you see?

- Consider writing a spiritual mission or vision statement for your youth ministry. Use this statement to evaluate how each individual element of your ministry works for or against your intended vision.

chapter 3
what is missional youth ministry?

Brian

Original Blog Date: July 2

Last week was our annual youth mission trip. Overall the trip was a success. We gathered with 450 youth from around the country. Lives were changed, tears were shed, God was present, and we bonded as a group. I could spend several posts talking about all of the different aspects of a youth mission trip. But then it happened. We returned home. Now all of us, myself included, are coming down from the mission trip "high."

I wish every day could be a day full of inspirational actions and life-changing events. I wish every day (well, maybe not every single day) I could gather around the cafeteria tables with my youth and share a meal while listening to them talk about what's on their hearts and minds. I wish each night could end with group devotions.

What happens when you and your teenagers are all pumped up from a mission trip and you return to the real world? How do we keep our youth continually engaged and cognizant of the fact that how we behave during one week should be the way we behave throughout the entire year? Perhaps we need to spend more time recognizing the ways in which we practice our faith the other 51 weeks of the year. . . . What if we spent a year doing missions in our hometowns? What would our youth groups look like then? —Jacob

In my very first year as a youth minister, I angered a whole group of adults in my church. I wanted to make one little change in the programming: trade the annual youth group ski trip for a youth group mission trip. I assumed everyone would love the idea of our teenagers spending a week of their summer vacation helping the needy, rather than spending a week of their Christmas vacation skiing the slopes. I was wrong.

Meetings were called. Letters were written. I was "invited" to meet with the adults on the youth council and explain why I was taking away this important event. It was then explained to me that the ski trip attracts lots of new teens to the church. Wasn't that our mission? I countered that mission trips also attract new people and wasn't serving others a part of our mission, too? We were at an impasse. What was the mission of our ministry together: to attract teenagers to our church and its particular expression of the gospel or to take the gospel out into the world by caring for the needs of others?

What Does It Mean to Be Missional?

Twenty years have passed since that disagreement, and the debate over how we define *mission* in the church continues. A wonderful teacher of mine was fond of saying, "The church does not do mission. The church is mission." If this is true, then as we seek to develop missional youth ministries, one of the challenges before us will be to define what *missional* means.

Sit down with five youth workers and—depending on the youth workers' theological leanings (evangelical? progressive? conservative? mainline?) and the desires of the particular faith communities they serve—you'll likely receive five different definitions of *mission*. When I speak with youth workers, some describe mission as being volunteer activities, such as building a house or feeding homeless people. Others describe mission as opportunities to go preach the gospel and convert people to Christianity.

In the mainline church, we're more likely to refer to the first example as *mission* and the second as *evangelism*. And I think it's fair to say that in the mainline church we don't put near as much emphasis on evangelism as our more evangelical brothers and sisters—at least not the kind of evangelism that involves asking people, "Do you accept Jesus Christ as your Lord and Savior?" In mainline youth ministry, mission experiences tend more toward the St. Francis model: "Preach the Gospel at all times and when necessary use words." It's the difference between a *tell* approach to mission and a *show* approach to mission. So how about a *show-and-tell* approach? Is it one or the other, both, or something else altogether?

At its most basic level, we might define *mission* as "that which gives expression to the relationship between God and the church and God and the world." Mission could be seen as God's self-revelation to the world. That's a lot to chew on, and therein lies the reason why it's so difficult to define *mission*. The mission of God isn't wholly ours to comprehend. It will always be, to some degree, indefinable—just as God is indefinable. But what we *can* define is our part in that mission. As we serve young people, we can strive to help teens understand their part in God's mission of transforming the world through the sharing of justice, peace, love, and saving grace.

The Risks of Following Jesus

But before we involve youth in this mission of God, let's consider how risky such an activity might be—for them and for us. Recall the reaction Jesus received when he visited his hometown and dared to suggest that God's mission was working itself out through him:

> When he came to Nazareth, where he had been brought up, he went to the synagogue on the sabbath day, as was his custom. He stood up to read, and the scroll of the prophet Isaiah was given to him. He unrolled the scroll and found the place where it was written:
>
> > "The Spirit of the Lord is upon me,
> > because he has anointed me

> to bring good news to the poor.
> He has sent me to proclaim release to the captives
> and recovery of sight to the blind,
> to let the oppressed go free,
> to proclaim the year of the Lord's favour."

And he rolled up the scroll, gave it back to the attendant, and sat down. The eyes of all in the synagogue were fixed on him. (Luke 4:16-20 NRSV)

Here Jesus declares that God's mission includes solidarity with those who suffer and are in need. Sounds good, right? Yet, shortly after proclaiming these words, Jesus' hometown folk tried to throw him off a cliff! But that doesn't stop him. We know Jesus will not only proclaim this mission, but also live it out. Jesus will bring good news to the poor, release those in captivity, restore sight to the blind, and grant freedom to the oppressed. His part in God's mission will involve *both* declaring the gospel in word and living it out in deeds of life-transforming love. And we know that doing so will eventually get him killed.

When we invite our youth to take part in the mission of God, do we understand that this is the sort of radical and dangerous mission to which we're calling them to commit their lives? Wouldn't it be safer to stay in the comfort of our youth rooms and just talk about mission?

Original Blog Date: September 17

My old ritual, as youth group wrapped up on Sunday evenings and the young'ns were heading home, was to say to them, "Be safe." Isn't that a strange way to say good-bye? Of course, all I meant was, "Have a good week and come back in one piece." But is that really the best advice we have to give to our youth? They live in a world of school violence, sexually transmitted diseases, drugs, computer predators, and even terrorism. Is being safe all that it's cracked up to be? What about when it comes to our faith? Is teaching our youth to "play it safe" our best option? Probably not, but are we willing to lead youth ministries that encourage real risk? —Brian

This conversation always brings to mind one of my favorite passages in C. S. Lewis' book *The Lion, the Witch and the Wardrobe*. While chatting with the young protagonists of the story, Mr. and Mrs. Beaver are trying to describe Aslan, the Lion who rules the kingdom of Narnia. Young Lucy, taken aback by the notion of meeting a lion, asks if he's safe. Mr. Beaver replies that of course he isn't safe. But he is good.

I find that too often our youth ministries offer a Jesus who is safe, a Jesus who asks little of us beyond giving intellectual assent to a list of religious beliefs. We give our teenagers a Jesus who says, "Just agree that I'm your Lord and Savior, and then I'll leave you alone to your video game nights and your road trips and your skateboard parks." We know that for the early church, following Jesus wasn't just about committing to a list of do's and don'ts, or pledging allegiance to religious dogma. For them, following Jesus meant walking through life the way he walked—and taking on all the risks that living this way would invite. Living as a disciple wasn't primarily about abstract belief but about a way of being in the world.

If we dare to call teenagers to this way of being and living and loving, then we'd better be prepared for trouble. Because following Jesus with our youth—*really* following Jesus—will be anything but safe. Here's what it could look like:

- Radically rethinking the environment we create—even though it's an environment in which we're pretty comfortable. Do our youth rooms really need a mini fridge, big screen TV, and an Xbox? What would happen if we sold all of that stuff and gave the money to the needy?
- Letting go of all our old distinctions of rich and poor, male and female, young and old, powerful and powerless, respected and shamed, cool and uncool, popular and unpopular. Which young people are missing from our youth ministries because they don't think they'd be welcome in the church? What are we doing to extend the hand of Christian hospitality to these people?
- Opposing violence and working for peace. Do we dare plan a protest march on behalf of abuse victims or refugees? Do we dare stand up for the oppressed in our communities?
- Speaking out against intolerance and injustice and calling on the

45

church to do the same. Do our teens understand the intersection of their faith and their attitudes about health care, poverty, AIDS, abortion, the death penalty, and racism?

- Leaving the comfort of our churches to go out and literally feed the poor, clothe the naked, care for the lonely, and heal the sick. What would happen if we did this every week and not just on the annual mission trip?
- Deciding that sharing our faith requires more than just convincing other people of our religious point of view. What would it look like for our teens to live out the radical love of Jesus in the halls of their schools? In their families? In their neighborhoods?

None of this stuff is safe. Some of it is so risky that it would require us to completely transform our ministries into something unrecognizable. Some of our teens will jump at the chance to be a part of this radical living out of the gospel, to be world changers. Some will leave and find a youth group that's more entertaining and less challenging. Some will stick with a safe version of Jesus, rather than follow a Jesus who calls us to overturn the tables of the world and work for something completely different.

If you're not sure whether your ministry is following the radical Jesus or just playing it safe, ask yourself this: *Is my ministry meeting any resistance from people—youth and adults—who are happy with the cultural status quo?* If you're playing it safe to keep your job, or to make sure your teens like you, or to make parents happy, then it's time to flip everything you're doing upside down.

Finding Your Mission Field

All of this talk about taking risks brings us back around to the question we started with: *Is mission about proclaiming the good news by our words or demonstrating the good news by our deeds?* The example set by Jesus clearly tells us it's both.

Given this understanding, just about any activity, any study, any program, or any event we engage in with young people can be considered mission—as long as we remember that our ministries exist not only for our own faith formation, but also for those who aren't yet a part of the fellowship of the faith community. Any activity we do with teenagers can be considered mission if we remember that our call is to reach out and share the good gifts of God's love with others. And more often than not, that call is going to take us beyond the doors of our youth rooms.

Oh, we'll still gather weekly for study, worship, and fellowship. But if we're truly committed to creating missional youth ministry, we'll realize that those times spent cloistered together in our churches are meant to recharge our batteries, refine our spiritual gifts, and fire up our passion to spend the rest of the week out in the mission field of God's world.

As important as it is to gather inside the walls of the youth room to tell and retell the story of new life in Christ, it's even more important to respond to Jesus' call to live out that story on the mission field. Now for the surprise: that mission field is right outside the door.

Original Blog Date: August 16

My church has a 20-plus-year history of taking their youth all over the country for summer choir tours and mission trips. More than a year ago, the young people at the church latched onto the idea of going to Mexico for their summer mission experience. In their typically enthusiastic way, the teenagers chose a location long before they asked what kind of work they would do when they got there or even where their efforts might be needed. We put the project on the back burner for a while, partly because I was fairly new to the church and wasn't ready yet to take on such a bold project.

More recently the teens raised the issue again, and I gave it some real thought. *Could we put such a project together? Could we afford it? Was it a good use of the church's mission funds? Would it be a good experience for our youth and those they might serve?* As all these questions swirled about, I happened to attend the Princeton Theological Seminary Institute for Youth Ministry in Seattle. While I was there, I had the opportunity to spend an afternoon serving at a local church that provides a hot-meal ministry to homeless teens. The ministry began about 10 years ago when the church's junior high youth group decided to use their mission trip money to help people in their own backyard. They opened this summer soup kitchen, and it's still going strong, serving meals seven days a week. —Brian

Inspired by this story, I returned to my church and presented the youth group with a challenge: "I know we want to go to Mexico next summer. So what if we spend some time *this* summer helping ministries right here in St. Louis?" With the idea out on the table, I waited for the inevitable protests. But they didn't come. Instead, the teenagers asked questions and wanted to know how this would work. Before long, we'd made our decision.

We started planning a summer mission experience that helped our youth see the needs of our city. And then for one week of that summer, we worked, ate, played, and prayed together in our own hometown while visiting with the elderly, working in soup kitchens, painting at an inner-city school, and lending a hand in homeless shelters. The youth saw parts of the city they'd never visited before—and probably never would have visited if they hadn't been willing to hear Christ's call to serve the least of these right in their very midst.

This experience was like a smack upside the head, telling me, *Do you get it now? Mission begins right here—not after you travel thousands of miles to some other state or country. God is calling you to serve in your own backyard.* Before we start thinking about mission trips to exotic locales like Mexico, Africa, or even Pittsburgh, we need to hear the cries coming from our own streets, our own alleys, our own contexts.

In fact, if we're going to create missional youth ministries, maybe we should all tattoo the word *context* on our arms. Missional youth ministry means constantly asking ourselves questions such as, *What is our context? What are the needs of our neighborhoods, our schools, our homes, and our town? What are the places and people right under our noses who need to hear about and experience the overwhelming grace and love of God?*

This is where things start to get dangerous again because in order to answer those questions, we have to become keenly aware of what little time we have with these young people: just a few hours a week over the course of several years, if that. So there's no time to waste. We don't have the luxury of running youth ministries that spend 50 percent of their time entertaining teens with ski trips and bowling tournaments and laser tag, while slipping in mission work when the kids aren't paying attention.

Don't get me wrong. I'm not knocking the importance of fellowship in a youth program. (In fact, we'll deal with building relationships more thoroughly in chapter 4.) Without a doubt fellowship can be meaningful, evocative of the Christian faith, and spiritually connected to God's mission. For example, rather than sending several groups out on a scavenger hunt to take photos of themselves all stuffed inside a phone both or cramming donuts into their mouths, they could take creative and thoughtful images of such things as peace, love, Christ, and "do unto others." Instead of having a night of Olympics-style competitive challenges, sponsor a Kingdom Olympics where the goal is to perform random acts of kindness out in the community, and the key is cooperation instead of competition. Make every moment an opportunity for them to participate in the way of Christ. Make every moment a chance for them to get a glimpse of the kingdom of God.

I'm not suggesting that you never take a mission trip to a far-off locale. But I do want to say loud and clear that I believe the mission field begins in the church parking lot and there's no better place to help young people find their place in the kingdom of God than in their own backyards. Because it's familiar territory, your local community is the perfect place for teenagers to uncover their gifts for ministry and to develop their ability to see the great, deep needs of the world. Serving close to home can open young people's eyes to the cries of God's children in other parts of the world as well.

Redefining Our Mission

I know firsthand the power of a mission trip. I first felt called to ministry while I was on a mission trip many years ago. I was with my church youth group serving in some low-income neighborhoods in Tampa. One day we were asked to go to a local daycare center and do some painting. As it turned out, it was difficult to get much work done because the children were literally hanging on us. They were hungry for attention and affection.

We quickly realized that our ministry had much less to do with paint and much more to do with presence. It was a transformative experience for me, and it led to my eventual studies in child development and my first career (and ministry) as an elementary school teacher. I fully believe mission trips can transform lives and provide space for young people to hear God's call.

What I'm really asking us to think about is our whole idea of mission. It's about more than where we go or what kind of work we do. Mission is more than an event. I believe it needs to be what defines our ministry to youth.

Original Blog Date: May 21

What if we stopped organizing youth mission trips? How long have youth mission trips been a must-have ingredient to successful youth programs? Certainly as long as I've been in youth ministry. In fact, one of my most memorable experiences of youth group as a teen was a mission trip during my senior year of high school.

Every summer youth groups spread out across the country to sample an experience of hands-on mission. For many groups these trips are seen as great ways to draw group members closer together, build lasting memories, and provide teenagers with a chance to see what it's like to help those in need. But are these trips actually helpful in launching youth into lifelong mission? —Brian

Let's consider for just a moment the possible downside of youth mission trips:

- Since these trips are taken by teenagers and a few adult leaders, they encourage age segregation within the church. That further distances young people from the wider church family.
- Summer mission trips, usually a week or two in length, can encourage an understanding of mission as being a once-a-year effort and something that happens far from home, rather than a constant attitude and awareness of the mission we're called to be a part of every day.
- Many churches entice youth to go on mission trips with promises of detours to amusement parks, tourist sites, shopping malls, and a fancy dinner at the end of the week. (Could this be an attempt to leave

behind *the least of these* and reintegrate ourselves back into middle-class culture?) Such enticements distract teenagers from the true purpose of mission and feed into the consumerist mentality of feeling we must get something in return for our efforts to help others.

- There is a stewardship issue inherent in youth mission trips. Depending on the amount of work the youth will do over the course of the trip, the costs of such trips can be quite expensive. In some cases, it would be a better act of stewardship to forgo spending money on travel, food, and lodging and instead donate the same amount to the mission organization or effort you wish to support.

The shift from a mission trip mindset to a missional ministry mindset will impact more than just your youth group. It will carry your whole church to new ways of thinking and being. Imagine what would happen in your church and your community if you started with a new set of assumptions about mission. What would happen if—

- We moved from youth mission trips to intergenerational missional experiences where everyone in the church is invited to participate?
- For every trip across the country or to Mexico, youth groups organized local mission efforts?
- Instead of short bursts of mission work in the summer, our youth ministries adopted long-term mission projects, such as working regularly in local homeless shelters or volunteering weekly in nursing homes or organizing ongoing peace and justice efforts?
- We shifted our ministry budgets so that most of our funds went not toward new sound equipment or new furniture for the youth room, but toward meeting the needs of our communities and spreading the good news of the gospel?
- We turned our churches, our fellowship rooms, and our youth lounges into mission centers—places where other groups could stay while they join us in mission work right in our hometowns?

If we're willing to risk seeing mission this way, then mission trips to other places simply become part of a year-round awareness of the part we play in God's ongoing transformation of the world. Of course, such a shift will also call for changes in the way we conduct our mission experiences as we put the focus where it rightly belongs: on God and God's community, rather than our own individual needs and desires.

To achieve this shift toward a more meaningful and Spirit-filled mission experience, I suggest the following guidelines:

Lose the technology. You can't imagine what a difference it makes while driving those long highway hours if you make teens and adults put away their personal listening devices and cell phones and actually spend time talking to each other, singing, playing car games, and enjoying the passing sights. This doesn't mean you have to ban the electronics altogether. Just restrict them to rest and sleep times when it makes sense for everyone to be off in their own little worlds.

Focus on the work. Help your young people see that work, particularly in the service of others, can be fun and should be enticement enough—without the promise of an amusement park at the end. There are plenty of small ways to make the week fun and build fellowship. Share meals together. Go out for ice cream. Take in a free local historical spot as the setting for your evening devotions. Play games. If you have time on the way home for an impromptu fun stop, then by all means stop. But let the call of God be the reason the youth choose to participate, not the call of the amusement park.

Be flexible. After 20 years of doing mission trips, I can tell you they never come off the way you plan. You can go over every last detail in advance and spend months getting organized, only to find out that the rental company doesn't have your vans ready on time, or the mission site has booked too many groups for the week, or the adult whom you expected to be the biggest help turns out to have a grumpy streak a mile wide. In my experience teenagers are much better at dealing with last-minute changes than adults are. So prepare everyone to expect the unexpected, go with the flow, and regularly repeat this word like a sacred mantra: *flexibility!*

Meet God in those you serve. This goes without saying, I suppose, but it's such an important lesson. We go to serve and to be examples of God's love to others, only to be met by an even deeper and more profound faith in the people we're helping. On a recent mission trip to the Gulf Coast, my group planned to spend the week eating peanut butter and jelly sandwiches on the worksite. But then we discovered that the woman whose mobile home we were rehabbing planned to treat us to home-cooked Cajun food every day! These lunches together gave us an opportunity to really get to know our host and for her to witness to us about her faith in the face of the trials she'd experienced during and after Hurricane Rita. Her witness to us was a powerful reminder that even as we go out to share God with others, we shouldn't forget that God is already there waiting to greet us.

Let the day begin and end with prayer. Sometimes the group can get so caught up in the work that they forget to center themselves. On a recent trip, a few teenagers in our group were so anxious to get to the worksites in the morning that they took off without joining the rest of us for prayers and devotion time. Likewise, some of the group members were so bent on buying supplies for the next day's work that they opted for an evening trip to Home Depot and skipped out on the evening devotions. It's crucial to begin and end the day with a focus on God and the path of Christ that calls one to mission in the first place. During the hectic schedule of the week of work, it reminds us of who we are and *whose* we are.

Resist thinking it's all about you. Humbly engaging in mission means remembering we're just part of God's work in the world. God was at work in that mission site before your group arrived, and God will be at work there long after you leave. Don't burden yourself (or fool yourself) by thinking that if you don't get the work done, then no one will! Bring along a good dose of humility, do what you can, and trust that God's ways of love and peace will continue in that place even after you return home.

The Big Picture

Looking back at that church fight over whether the youth group should take a mission trip or a ski trip, I realize we were all missing the big picture. The question isn't whether this activity or that activity is mission. Mission isn't something we program, nor is it something we control. It's not about numbers and it's not about feeling good about ourselves. Mission can and should encompass all that we do. It's a daily, moment-by-moment opportunity to step into the work of God and be a part of God's way of peace, justice, mercy, and compassion. Inviting youth into that mission is risky and possibly even dangerous, and we should realize how blessed we are to be a part of that work in the kingdom of God.

Jacob's Reflections

I love mission trips. What other chance do you get to spend an entire week with a group of teens and adult sponsors worshipping, working, eating, and serving? But mission trips aren't always easy. In fact mission trips are some of the most difficult aspects of youth ministry. Not only do you have to do all of the planning, but you also have the experience of what it's like to spend a week with your teenagers—true characteristics are revealed. You really gain a sense of what it means to be a community of Christ.

Halfway through a mission trip, I inevitably get the following question from both youth and adults: "With all of the money we raised and spent to get here, couldn't we have just hired a professional to do a more effective job? Is this trip really worth it?" The answer to this question is a resounding yes! I believe the mission trip is worth all of the costs and logistics, and here's why: If you raised some money and had somebody else do the job, it probably could be done more efficiently and even at a cheaper cost. But then you'd lose a unique opportunity to gain the experience of what it means to serve others. You'd lose a chance to move beyond your comfort zone and away from the distractions of your daily life to learn firsthand the teachings of Jesus and the admonition that it's better to give than to receive. You'd miss out on possibilities of creating deep, lifelong relationships within your ministry. You'd lose out on the experience of worshipping with one another for several days at a time, experiencing both the highs and lows of mission work.

I share Brian's vision that mission is the church. The church is mission. And I agree that you don't have to travel far away in order to create a unique mission experience. When I first started as a youth minister, I made sure to take mission trips that involved long van rides and lots of entertainment along the way. I thought this was the most effective way to create community. Looking back on it now, I believe this was a mistake.

Unconsciously, at least during the first several years, I created an institutional memory that mission trips must involve going out of town. If I had a chance to change the way we do mission trips—and we hope to move in this direction—I'd alternate between having in-town mission trips and out-of-town trips. It would be a good experience to have a mission trip in the city where we live, serve others within the community, and stay at the church for a week—just like we would anywhere else. Of course the challenge would be for everyone involved, both youth and parents, to realize that an in-town mission trip is still a weeklong commitment that cannot be divided between sporting activities, family events, and other commitments.

Brian began this chapter by sharing his struggle with defining the term *mission*. Before you leave for a mission trip, why not take the time to share that same struggle with your youth ministry? Through both conversation and worship, discern together your understanding of mission. Discuss openly the differences between a mission trip and making a commitment to be missional. Create a covenant with one another to commit to your vision of mission, remembering why we serve and who we serve as disciples of Christ.

As we come to expand our understanding of mission beyond just isolated events, mission will be to our youth ministries as oxygen is to our bodies—with it we have life, without it we cease to exist. When our young people come to understand our ministries as missional instead of programmatic or entertainment-focused, they'll begin to see that they can embody the good news of the gospel in their schools, neighborhoods, families, and with their friends. Imagine what could happen if Christian teens were empowered to see themselves as missionaries—not just during the annual mission trip, but all year round.

Rethinking Your Own Ministry

- Meet with a group of adult and student leaders to help you define the word *mission*. How does your team's understanding of mission compare or contrast with the stated or implied mission of your church?

- Are you taking risks for mission in your ministry with youth? What could be holding you back? Where might God be calling you to be more *dangerous* in your missional activities?

- What are the needs of the neighborhood in which your church is located? How might you engage youth in addressing those concerns?

- Consider the teens you serve. What unique gifts do they have for mission? How might you use these gifts in your own neighborhood or city?

- Before you start planning your next mission trip, sit down with your group and pose the question: "Why should we take this trip?" See how many answers you can brainstorm together.

chapter 4
building real relationships

Jacob

Several years ago I started receiving emails from colleagues saying: "Help! I've taken a new position with the church, and my primary responsibility is working with the youth group. I have no idea what I'm doing. How do I begin?" While I always find such emails a little humorous, I can completely relate. I remember having the same exact feeling: *Where to start? What to do?*

The good news is it will be okay—particularly if we let go of the idea that we're tasked first and foremost with creating and maintaining an endless youth ministry calendar crammed full of activities. Before we put one Bible study, one game night, one mission project on the schedule, we need to stop and contemplate a key word: *relationships.*

Jesus didn't spend his time scheduling entertaining and excitement-fueled programs for his disciples or followers. A quick scan of the Gospels paints a portrait of Jesus' ministry as one defined by his relationships with others. Each time we see Jesus, he's taking the time to hear and see others in their entirety. He listens to those whose voices are ignored. He stops to speak with those who are considered outcasts. He not only calls people to his side, but also takes the time to seek them out on their own turf.

In the Gospel of Luke, we read how Zacchaeus climbs a tree just to get a glimpse of Jesus as the mob passes. But it's Jesus who stops, calls to Zacchaeus, and invites himself to lunch at the home of this despised tax collector. And this time spent with Jesus transformed the man's life; Zacchaeus was never the same.

In story after story, Jesus' interactions with people offer a powerful reminder of the potential for experiencing God through relationships. Without a doubt Jesus is fully present when ministering to individuals: the poor, the hungry, children, outcasts, and those yearning to know God intimately. And our lives are lived to their fullest potential when we recognize the presence of Christ in one another.

As those who work with youth, we carry the incredible responsibility of being representatives of Christ to the teenagers in our ministries. How we relate to them, make (or don't make) an effort to listen to them, spend time with them, and try to understand them has the potential to have a tremendous impact on how they perceive God and Christ.

The strategies I suggest below will be helpful for anyone who's working in youth ministry—from volunteers to paid staff. The ultimate goal for all of us in using these strategies is to be fully present with our young people and develop relationships within our ministries that reflect Christ's radical love.

Original Blog Date: October 22

Three years ago, when I started serving Broadway Christian Church, I spent a lot of time forming relationships with the young people. I felt that before I could do any significant planning or discern the future of the youth ministry, I needed to know each teenager as well as I could. I focused on five ways to kick-start these relationships:

1. I either called or went to the home of all the teenagers and personally invited them to youth group.
2. I took pizza to their schools and joined them—and their friends—for lunch.

3. I sent each person in the group a personalized birthday card made from my cereal boxes.
4. I prayed for and with each person in the group.
5. I made sure the group members knew I was always available to chat, email, pray, or just hang out.

I spend a lot of time meeting with teens in schools, talking on the phone, emailing, and visiting. But I'm always looking for new methods of relationship building. —Jacob

Building Relationships Face-to-Face

Think back a moment to your own days in middle school and high school and how important relationships were in your life: friends, teachers, coaches, family members, youth ministers. In many cases these relationships helped us become the people we are today.

Adolescence is the time when people begin experimenting with the identity they want to have as adults. Friends act as a sort of social mirror helping young people see themselves through the eyes of others. That's why friendships during the teenage years become more important and more intense than they are in childhood. Teens are likely to seek out those with similar interests and values or join social groups that seem new and different as a way of trying on new identities to see if they fit.

Just as friendships with peers provide a sort of social mirror in the present, teenagers seek relationships with adults as a way of figuring out what kind of people they might become. As teenagers begin the process of individuating and seeking some distance from their parents, relationships with other adults (such as teachers and youth leaders) become even more important. These interactions allow teens to role-play what adult relationships look and feel like and begin to imagine the sorts of meaningful relationships they eventually want to have with friends and co-workers and spouses.

That's why those of us in youth ministry should never underestimate the crucial role that relationships play for our teenagers. Even when we're tired of the ever-changing circles of friends, the drama of who's mad at whom and why, the compulsive need our teens have to talk to each other and spend time together, we have to remember that all of this is part of their normal development. Our job is to help them build healthy, lasting relationships with one another, with adults, and with God.

When I first arrived at my current church, there weren't many opportunities for teenagers to make meaningful connections. There had never been a youth group that met on Sunday nights, so I was more than a little apprehensive about the response I'd get for a weekend gathering.

My initial plan was to visit every youth group member at home so I could learn a bit about each one of them, get their ideas for the group, and meet the parents. But when that proved too ambitious for me, I decided to at least call all of them. I'd ask about their interests, find out how long they'd been attending the church, and talk about what they hoped to gain from the youth ministry. Some didn't talk much; but others spent a long time telling me about their faith, hopes, dreams, and interests. All of them seemed to appreciate receiving a personal phone call.

I learned a lot from that first year in youth ministry, and I continue to make relationship building my first priority. For some youth leaders, this kind of micro-level youth ministry feels like a waste of time. Or they're so busy planning the next big activity that they don't have time for the slow process of nurturing relationships. I know it can seem overwhelming to make that personal connection with every person in your group. But I've got a few tried-and-true methods for getting to know my teens.

Each fall I have the teenagers in my youth group fill out a brief questionnaire called "All About You." The questions are simple: name, age, grade, school, hobbies, sports, lunch hour, cell phone, email, and parents' names. I've found that if I know this basic information, I'm in a better position to start building individual connections with each teen. It's an effective means of building the foundation of a relationship.

I also continue to use the Zacchaeus model and meet teenagers on their own turf. I bring pizza to their schools and spend a lunch hour with them and their friends. There's no agenda; it's just a time to talk, laugh, and stay connected. I also spend a fair amount of time at basketball games, track meets, school plays and musicals, band concerts, and football games. When I go to each of these events, I may talk to whoever is participating for just a few minutes. But my presence says a lot. Months—even years—later, I've had young people tell me how much they appreciated my coming to their track meet or volleyball game.

Whether you have a group of 5 or 105 teenagers, it would be a mistake to take the Lone Ranger approach to connecting with them. Don't assume you can be all things to all young people by attending every sporting event, play, and concert. Instead, it's important to develop a team of caring adults who are willing to connect with youth beyond your weekly program and activities. These extra interactions can be crucial for helping your fellow leaders develop trust and connection with teenagers.

An adult volunteer's willingness to visit a young person on her own turf can be the beginning of a deeper relationship. When teens know you care about their whole lives and not just their participation at church, they'll be more willing to be open and honest with you about their deepest needs, greatest struggles, questions, and journey of faith.

Building Relationships Through Technology

If your youth group is like mine, you're finding it increasingly difficult to schedule one-on-one time with your teens. Their lives are so packed that even grabbing a cup of coffee or a slice of pizza with you can seem like one more obligation, rather than a chance to relax and chat.

That's where technology can help. In case you haven't noticed, teenagers live by their tech gadgets and applications. Facebook, texting, online chats, email, Twitter, cell phones—these are the ways teenagers connect with each other. And they're often their preferred means of connecting with adults as well.

While you shouldn't let virtual connections take the place of face time with your teens, you can make the most of their ready reliance on technology. If you're smart about it, technology can help strengthen your ministry as it allows you to stay caught up with the members of your youth group in ways that would have been impossible even five years ago.

I'd been on Facebook for only a few days when I realized how quickly and easily I could stay in touch with the teenagers in my group. Teens tend to overshare on sites such as Facebook, telling the world—or at least their Facebook friends—about every detail of their lives. Therefore, I know who's having a rough day, who's struggling with a decision, and who got the part in the play or that summer job we'd prayed about. It took me a while to get used to having this kind of access to their lives. Yet it's given me valuable insights about what they need from youth ministry.

This oversharing, however, has some interesting implications for youth ministry. While trying to get teens to talk about their lives during youth group can be incredibly frustrating, they freely share all sorts of information online. So what kind of community are they creating on the Web? Is it the kind of community Jesus envisioned?

Original Blog Date: August 18

Usually, even though we have mission trips and camps, I don't stay as connected with my youth group over the summer. But this year that has really changed. Facebook has totally reinvented the ways in which I maintain my relationships with young people. It seems like everyone, all day long, constantly gives updates on what they're doing. It really is amazing. But my question is this: Can you maintain a sense of community over status updates? The answer: I'm not sure.

As we begin planning for our community-building activities this fall, I wonder what the role of technology will be. Sometimes it seems that youth share more openly on Facebook than they do in person. What does this say about our level of comfort with one another? Can we only say what we really think when we're in the comfort of cyberworld?

What is the balance between Facebook and youth group? Facebook and church? —Jacob

I appreciate the ways in which social media has allowed me to connect with others, particularly the teenagers I serve. I have a good sense of what they experience and feel on a daily basis. Yet their willingness to share such personal information online encourages me to ask questions: *Is there a fear among our young people that they can't be as genuine at youth group as they are online? Do Internet communities either create or reveal our true identities?*

These questions became more than an academic discussion several years ago when a young girl in our area committed suicide because of messages that had been posted on her MySpace page. In an effort to understand how this had happened, our youth group had a conversation about what it means to build relationships over the Internet.

After a few introductory games and activities, we listed all the ways we form our identities. Then we looked at identity from a biblical perspective. We talked about the reasons someone might portray one identity at school and something totally opposite at home or online. That led us to an honest conversation about our need to feel affirmed and liked and how that desire can sometimes lead people to pretend to be someone other than who they really are.

I came away from that conversation with the reminder that teenagers have a strong desire to try on different identities. In the midst of that process, they need to know others truly care for them and will stick with them as they figure out who they are. I was also reminded that when things go bad and teens feel there's no one to turn to, the situation can become disastrous very quickly. This is why it's crucial that the church be a place in which teenagers experience Christlike relationships where everyone is accepted—particularly the outsiders—and can find a friend who's ready to listen.

Adult-Teen Boundaries and Youth Ministry

Even as we acknowledge the importance of adult-teen relationships in youth ministry, it's equally important to consider the need for boundaries in such relationships. The church carries a particularly heavy burden in this area as our relationships are expected to reflect the nature of God's love. How we interact with young people can have a powerful and long-lasting effect on their faith development.

Original Blog Date: October 20

A teenager asks to speak with you about a personal problem. You agree to meet with him or her in your office at the church after school. The teen comes in, you close the door to have a private conversation, and 15 minutes later the church sec-

retary goes home—leaving you alone in the building with a teenager. You may have just made the biggest mistake of your youth ministry career.

I know that in my earliest years in youth ministry, when I was 20-something, I didn't give a great deal of thought to personal boundaries when it came to the young people I was serving. I thought I was really doing my job when I had opportunities to meet with them one-on-one, to visit them in their homes, to talk with them on the phone. I was a youth director—a lay leader in a paid church position—with none of the expectations of having to do periodic boundary training like a licensed or ordained pastor. But in the ensuing years, I became more educated on just how easy it is for adult leaders and young people alike to cross boundaries—social boundaries, personal boundaries, sexual boundaries, ethical boundaries. There are situations that were commonplace in my early days of ministry that I wouldn't even consider putting myself into today. —Brian

Thinking intentionally about the boundaries in adult-teen relationships isn't optional. We have to be prepared to help all the adults in our youth ministries understand how to interact with youth in ways that are safe, nurturing, and avoid even the appearance of impropriety. We suggest the following as the most basic of guidelines anytime you interact with youth:

Require multiple adults. Be certain to have at least two adults present and within sight of each other at all times whenever adults are interacting with teenagers in your ministry. This is nonnegotiable in our opinion. In a time of heightened awareness of abuse by clergy, it's paramount that young people (no matter what age) not be alone with an adult. Of course, this rule also protects adults from being accused of something improper or having their actions misinterpreted by a young person.

Does this mean you can't meet one-on-one with a teenager? No, but it does mean you can't be alone with one. We often arrange to meet young people at a local coffeehouse or restaurant so there are other people present. If you meet with teens in your office, insist that the door have a window so others can easily see you. If you must drive a teenager somewhere or take her home after youth group, bring another adult with you. Same-gender situations aren't exempt from this rule: Male leaders shouldn't be alone with boys, and female leaders shouldn't be alone with girls. No adult should be alone with a young person—regardless of the genders involved.

Practice safe touch. This one is tough for many youth leaders, particularly if you're a hugger. Let's be clear: There's nothing wrong with physical contact. Jesus often demonstrated the healing power of touch. But when it comes to teens and adults, there have to be boundaries. Encourage both youth and adults to focus on safe touch, which can include a pat on the back, a sideways hug (hip to hip with an arm around the shoulder), high-fives, handshakes, and A-frame hugs (where two people lean in and hug but their torsos aren't in contact). The most important question to ask when engaging in physical touch with teens is this: Do you want to offer touch to share God's love with the teen or do you need the physical contact yourself? What's your real motivation?

What if the teen is the hugger? What if the teen is seeking physical affection from you? Some young people naturally show love and care to others by way of touch—either because they've been raised that way, they explore their world through touch, or they haven't developed appropriate physical boundaries with other people. We don't want to send the message that this sort of behavior is wrong. At the same time, it's crucial that adults maintain clear physical boundaries—between teenagers and adults, as well as between teenagers.

The simplest way to approach this issue with teens is simply to be honest and use a little humor. Demonstrate safe touch practices for the whole group and let them practice together. See who can come up with the most creative way to do a high-five. Award a prize to the pair who can perform the most awkward A-frame hug. Challenge your teens to form a whole-group sideways hug. Laughing together as you practice safe touch will not only defuse any discomfort about the issue, but also reinforce that touch can be positive and affirming.

Foster transparency. As we've already mentioned, many of us utilize social networking as a way to stay connected with our youth group members. But the real danger here is transparency. We've heard of youth leaders who use the chat features on sites like Facebook to counsel teens. If you're a trained pastor, you might think there's no issue with this practice. But what about the other adults who work with you? Are they also having long private conversations with individual teens via chat or instant messaging? Do you have any way of accounting for these conversations?

The virtual world offers the same kinds of opportunities—and at least as many challenges—to youth ministry as face-to-face interactions. If you haven't already considered the kind of boundaries that you and your adult volunteers need to have for meeting with teenagers, it's time to figure that out. As you do, consider these issues of transparency:

- What kinds of interactions are appropriate outside of youth group? Counseling? Crisis intervention? Casual conversations? Do you have clear guidelines in place for when the youth pastor should be called into a situation?
- How should you track and account for these interactions? Should volunteers print out email exchanges and IM chats? Are there other steps you need to take to protect teens and adult volunteers?
- How would you deal with adult volunteers dating youth who are 18 or older? We firmly believe this type of relationship is inappropriate because the adult is in a position of authority over the teen. What youth protection policies do you already have in place that might address this issue? For example, if this occurs should the adult leader step down from a position of leadership?
- How should volunteers update you on outside conversations or meetings with teenagers?
- Do you run annual background checks on all adults working in your youth ministry?

Building Relationships Between Group Members

As important as it is for adults in the church to develop caring and Christ-like relationships with young people, it's equally important for us to help young people develop these sorts of relationships with each other. But let's be honest: It's difficult for teenagers to get to know each other very well while playing video games, watching a movie, or running around the neighborhood on a scavenger hunt. These sorts of activities can be an important part of developing fellowship in youth ministry, but only after you've established a solid foundation of care and trust.

The challenge is to help teenagers—who are prone to creating cliques and stereotyping their peers—invest the necessary time and energy to listen to and truly get to know one another. They need us to create an atmosphere of acceptance and openness that allows them to share their deeper thoughts and feelings.

We've found it helpful to start by talking about the connectedness of the faith community and our oneness as the body of Christ. The body metaphor works well with young people in church, but they often have a hard time translating the idea that they're still *one body* outside of the youth group.

Try this creative worship experience (designed to be used in early fall) to help encourage the group to stay connected all week long:

The Vine and the Branches Art Project

This art project will help your group think about what it means to be connected to each other both in and out of the youth group setting.

Prep: Cut leaf shapes from half sheets of construction paper. They don't have to be fancy, just a generic leaf shape will work. Make sure you have enough leaves for everyone in the group—adults included—plus some extras in case new people show up. On the night you do this activity, bring the leaves as well as plenty of crayons and markers.

Read: During the youth group gathering, have everyone sit in a circle and read John 15:1-11 out loud. This is the well-known text in which Jesus shares with his friends, "I am the vine; you are the branches. If a man remains in me and I in him, he will bear much fruit . . ." (John 15:5). Talk about what this image has to say about community and friendship. How can your group live this out?

Create: Pass out the leaves and have everyone grab a few crayons or markers. Each person should write his or her name on one side of the leaf. Next, ask them to draw a symbol on the other side of the leaf that reminds them of the group (it could be a heart, stick figure people, a cross, or anything else).

When everyone is finished, have them pass their leaves clockwise to the next person in the circle. This person should then write his or her name next to the first name on the leaf. Then ask a question and have each person write a short response on the other side of the leaf. Continue this process—passing the leaves, adding names, and responding to questions—until the leaves are back with their original owners.

You can ask any questions you'd like, but here are a few suggestions to get you started:

- Write a word to describe how you're feeling about your life right now.
- Write down something you're looking forward to in youth group this year.
- Draw a symbol or write a word or phrase describing how you feel about your relationship with God right now.
- List three things you're thankful for about this group.
- Write the name of at least one adult who's helped you experience God's love.
- List at least one thing you hope we do in youth group this year.
- List one class at school that you're excited about.
- List one class at school that you're dreading.
- Draw a symbol or write a word or phrase that describes something in your own life for which you'd like others to pray.
- Write the name of a person or place for which you hope others will pray.
- List one or more gifts or talents you could share with the group.

When everyone has received his or her original leaf, allow a few moments of silence for everyone to meditate on the responses and pray for the group. Encourage your teens to take their leaves home with them, post them someplace visible, and use them as daily touchstones to remind them to pray for each other and be mindful of their connection to their brothers and sisters in faith.

There are plenty of other ways for you to build relationships among your young people. Here are a few of our favorites:

Check-In
Rather than start each meeting with a high-energy game, put the focus on individuals by sitting in a circle and inviting each person to talk about her-

self for a minute or so. You might ask teens to share the high and low points of the past week, rate how they're feeling on a scale of 1 to 10, or describe where they encountered God's presence in the past few days.

Prized Possession

Prior to the meeting, ask group members to bring an object from home that represents their interests or personality—but ask them to keep their choices a secret. This object might be a favorite book, a toy, a shirt, or a CD of a favorite band. As people arrive at youth group, collect their items as covertly as you can.

Once everyone has arrived, spread out the items in the middle of the group. Select one item at a time and give the group three chances to figure out who brought it. When the group is done guessing, ask the owner to explain why that item represents who she is. If you have visitors or others who didn't bring an object, invite them to write a description of something they would have brought and include it with the pile.

Circle Sharing Time

This one is as simple as it gets, but it's so effective. Choose a new question each week and open your gathering by having everyone answer the question. Choose a question yourself or ask a teenager to come up with one. It could be something as simple as, "What's your favorite food?" or something more imaginative such as, "What time in history would you want to visit and why?" or "What's the greatest problem facing the world today?"

Affirmation Shower

This works best in small groups of no more than five people. One person from each group sits in a chair or on the floor as the rest of the group stands or sits in a circle around that person. When the group is ready, they begin to *shower* the person in the middle with affirmations, such as naming their gifts ("You're a good singer," "You're a great listener") or what they appreciate about the person ("You always smile," "You're a great friend," "You're really good at TPing people's houses!"). Each person in the group gets about a minute in the chair, and then another person gets a turn. It might sound corny, but this activity can be quite meaningful for both the person being showered and the rest of the group.

I Am Poems

Give each person a sheet of paper with the phrase I AM written 10 times down the left side of the paper. Pass out pencils and ask everyone to finish the phrase all the way down the paper. When they're done, explain that they've each created a poem that reveals something of themselves to the group. Invite those who are willing to share to read their poems out loud.

Offering Prayer

Close your meetings with a brief time of worship, asking each person to write down personal prayers on small sheets of paper. These prayers will be your offerings during worship. If you want to be a little more technological, you could have youth text their prayers to your phone or tweet them to a common Twitter account and then display their prayers on a screen. As each prayer is read, invite the group to respond, "God, in your love, hear our prayers."

Don't Stop Now

With these sorts of activities as a start, continue to build opportunities for your youth to develop more intimate and Christlike relationships with each other. Whatever the activity, the ultimate aim should be to create an environment where youth feel safe and free to be the people God created them to be.

Once your group has built a level of trust and connection, consider offering an event, such as a spiritual retreat, that's completely focused on relationship building.

Original Blog Date: October 21

Last weekend we had our annual boys' retreat. In the past we've always traveled to our local camp and conference center. This year we went on a two-night trip to a river in southern Missouri. While the nights were a little cold, the daytime temperatures were perfect. On the drive home, I reflected on our weekend retreat. I'm confident that outdoor retreats are a perfect opportunity—one that may not be possible anywhere else—to focus on God, creation, and community. The theme of the retreat was "Finding God in Nature." We spent time around the campfire talking about God's creation and how we're called to be stewards of the earth.

For almost 72 hours, I had a chance to live in community with my male youth and adult sponsors. We had no cell phone reception, no televisions, and no video games. Where else can you get this kind of opportunity for ministry? Sitting around the campfire, roasting marshmallows, chatting, and throwing buckeyes in the fire (yes, they do have impressive explosions) created memories that will last a lifetime. I encourage each of us to continually think of ways in which we can take our young people away from the busyness of their lives and provide them with the opportunity to slow down, relax, live in community, and celebrate the presence of God in their lives.

While on retreat we encourage the youth to spend time in silence, journal, and just appreciate the beauty of nature. Initially I didn't think a bunch of teenage boys would respond well to such suggestions. But I was completely wrong. I discovered that teenagers crave silence and nature. —Jacob

In addition to simply enjoying the silence, more than two years later the young men who went on that particular retreat still talk about the experiences of the weekend (including who flipped over whose canoe).

Whether it's over a pizza shared in a high school cafeteria or a weekend spent in contemplative retreat, the time we spend building loving, nurturing, Christlike relationships with young people creates space for them to learn and grow in faith. If we want teens to follow Jesus' way of love for one another, we have to be living examples of commitment and companionship.

Brian's Reflections

I remember two types of adults who worked with the youth group I attended in high school. There were those who sat in the back of the room while we had our Bible study or games or whatever the activity happened to be. We knew they were there, but they rarely got involved in what we were doing or engaged us in conversation. Then there were the adults who made a point of knowing what was going on in our lives both inside and outside of church. They kept up on what was happening with our families and what our plans were after high school, and they sought ways to help us become more involved in the ministries of the church. The relationships I formed with these caring adults are still important to me today, even if I rarely see them. The way they nurtured and mentored me as a young man continues to impact the way I try to guide the young people in my care. We never know what sort of lasting impact we might have.

In my own interactions with youth in the church, I've discovered that real spiritual growth is less likely to happen during the times when it's planned—for example, Bible study or large-scale events like Christian concerts. Meaningful spiritual formation comes when leaders are open to being present and willing to accept teenagers as they are, even while challenging them to grow and mature in their faith.

Certainly there's been some programming that's helped develop Christlike relationships between youth and adults. But more often these relationships deepen over a cup of coffee at the sandwich shop, or after a spontaneous sledding adventure on a school snow day, or when a teenager pulls a trusted adult aside after youth group and says, "I really need to talk to you about something." Teenagers can find entertainment and activity anywhere. They don't need us to give them more pizza, more video games, or more distractions. What they need from us is real, honest relationships that point them toward God.

Teenagers spend most of their time fighting off messages that tell them they aren't good enough and dealing with a culture that constantly judges them and pits them against one another. Youth ministry might be the one place in teenagers' lives where they experience God's unconditional love firsthand—if we're bold enough to share it with them.

Rethinking Your Own Ministry

- What relationships have played an important role in your faith formation?

- Consider what's taking priority in your youth ministry: programs or relationship building? Think back over your last two or three gatherings: What opportunities were there for youth and adults to build authentic relationships?

- How can you be even more intentional about developing relationships with the youth you serve?

- How does your ministry help young people create relationships with one another beyond your regular meetings?

- In 10 years what will your youth remember about their relationships with you or the other adults in your ministry?

chapter 5

purposeful planning

Jacob

I still remember my first morning as a youth leader. I walked into my new office, sat down, and had no idea what to do. It was a moment of acute culture shock and panic. Suddenly I realized I was responsible for developing and planning a successful youth ministry. During those first few months, my apprehension about planning and organizing continued to grow. I searched the Internet desperately and called friends and colleagues looking for ideas on developing a new youth ministry. What I'd come to realize was that while I was doing my best to plan for programming, I'd failed to plan for ministry.

We live in a results-and-success-oriented culture. Even the church has bought into the lie that its identity comes from its programs. We fill our church calendars with small-group meetings and potluck suppers, hayrides and family events—all in an effort to not only make ourselves attractive to those seeking a church, but also hold on to those who are already a part of our fellowship.

Many youth ministries have taken this same approach believing their success is determined by all the activities they've jammed into their monthly calendars. Program planning has its place. But so many of us spend far more time putting together events and activities than working to create a ministry in which youth and adults work together to discern who they're called to be as part of the church.

Original Blog Date: September 4

It occurred to me that many of us likely approach planning in very different ways. Some of us, out of necessity, do all the major planning ourselves, setting up a calendar of events for each month. Others work with adult volunteers and youth to jointly create a schedule of activities. Certainly one size does not fit all. Each ministry does what works best given its size and makeup of youth and adults.

I thought I'd share the basics of how we lay out the schedule in my program. We strive to have a rotation of meetings each month that looks like this:

Week One: Fellowship Activity
Week Two: Study/Discussion
Week Three: Mission Project
Week Four: Creative Worship

With good planning, and a little help from the Spirit, these activities are connected by a monthly theme, and each one helps the teens experience and think through the theme. If we're doing a study on "Where Is God in Your World?" we might start with a photo scavenger hunt for fun, inviting the youth to find images of God out in the community. The next week we dig into Scripture, studying images of God in the various texts. The following week we join together on a mission project that helps us be a part of God's work in the world. And in the final week we plan and lead a creative worship experience that draws together all the elements of our monthlong focus.

Now I know some youth ministers already have their entire school year planned out. They know what they're doing on the second Sunday of January of the following year. They already have a deposit down on a campground for the spring retreat, and they know where they're going for a mission trip next summer! Our group tends to be a little more spontaneous. I used to do a lot more advance planning, but I now take a more laid-back approach. I know where I think the group is heading between now and Christmas, but we leave plenty of room in the schedule to adapt based on what happens with the new group that comes together each fall. We take a less program-matic approach and allow the group to be organic—putting more focus on the growing of a caring community than on our activities. —Brian

After reading Brian's post, I began reflecting on the past few years and the journey I've taken as I've reassessed what it means to plan for ministry with youth. What follows might be considered my own personal odyssey of rethinking planning for youth ministry.

To Plan or Not to Plan

I admit that during my first year in youth ministry, I really didn't have a firm grasp on planning. I was blessed to enter a program where the adult sponsors had spent significant amounts of time scheduling activities and events for the upcoming year. Everyone involved with the youth ministry department knew definite dates for various retreats, mission trips, summer camps, service projects, and fellowship activities. What we didn't know for certain was how the schedule would look for the remaining calendar days.

While we had some great Sunday night meetings and special activities that first year, parents never knew a schedule more than a few weeks ahead of time (though they rarely complained). Every week, in my eagerness to be a fresh and energetic youth minister, I'd come up with a terrific new idea that I wanted our group to experience. The result of such spontane-ous brainstorming was that sometimes we'd meet during the middle of the week, sometimes on a Saturday, and sometimes on a Sunday. Sometimes we'd meet all weekend and sometimes not at all. By the end of the school year, I was lucky to have a group at all.

At the start of my second year, I knew we had to do things differently. The office manager was becoming a bit irritated that I never reserved space ahead of time or put events on the church calendar. The parents who were willing to volunteer said they'd like to know what was planned at least several months in advance so they could commit to the ministry and to the other important parts of their lives. And I knew I needed to have some long-term goals and expectations if I wanted to avoid burnout.

In the middle of June, I called a meeting of the adult volunteers, church department chairs, and the administrative assistant so we could plan the entire calendar for the following year. Our goal was to move beyond simply creating activities and focus on planning our ministry instead.

Like Brian's group, we wanted each month to include four basic elements: Bible study, worship, outreach, and fellowship. So we used that meeting to choose topics for each month, talk through the kinds of worship we wanted to experience, look into the mission projects we hoped to participate in, and narrow down a list of fellowship activities we wanted to do. Next, we created a master calendar for the entire year that we then gave to our volunteers and other members of the church staff. We sent out a monthly calendar to our youth and parents that provided a detailed schedule of all of the events and ministry opportunities taking place.

Thanks to this more thoughtful planning, my second year went fairly smoothly. I learned that if I knew what topics we were going to focus on several months (not days) ahead of time, I felt much better about my teaching and leadership.

But even with all of this advanced planning, I became keenly aware that I'd left out one important voice. It wouldn't remain that way for long.

Planning with Youth

One night after a particularly boring session, which I'd planned well ahead of time, several of the senior high students pulled me aside and said we needed to talk. As gently as they could, these teenagers let me know that I should have included them in the planning process. At first I was a little upset. After all, I'd spent a lot of time in my office preparing! I felt as though I knew what they needed better than they did. But by the time I got home that night, I knew they were right. We needed a youth leadership team.

Of course I'm not the first youth worker to learn this lesson the hard way. Many of us find it difficult to resist the Lone Ranger approach to planning. And there are certain advantages to guiding a youth ministry where you—and perhaps a small handful of adults—make all of the decisions. Such an approach can be efficient, simple, and relatively stress-free. You can be reasonably certain that adult leaders will follow through on their responsibilities, show up when they say they will, and follow your lead. But all of this can easily go out the window when we start involving youth in the process.

Original Blog Date: September 8

Our recent poll asked how you go about planning for fall programming. Sixty percent of you said you do all the planning yourselves. The second highest response was, "We don't do a lot of long-range planning. We like to be spontaneous!" Only a few folks said they work with others to do the planning.

I have to admit that it's easy for me to get into the habit of doing it all myself. On one level this makes sense. I'm the one who has time during the week to sit in my office and contemplate the best Bible studies, the right mixture of fellowship activities, the most effective schedule of lock-ins and retreats, and the most interesting mission projects. It's always easier and more efficient to just do it all myself. But imagine the benefits to the young people if they're brought into the planning process:

- Teenagers get the opportunity to think intentionally about ministry. They learn to be thoughtful about why you do what you do in your program. They develop the skill of discernment as they ask, "Is this the right activity or study or trip for us? Does it fit with who we are and what we're about as a youth group?"

- Teenagers get to see firsthand the amount of work that goes into keeping the ministries of a church moving ahead. They aren't insulated from the nuts and bolts, and this will help them develop into more thoughtful and effective leaders when they're involved in churches as adults. In other words, they'll understand that great programs and ministries don't happen by themselves!
- Teenagers develop ownership of their ministry and are better able to see their calling within that ministry. With luck, this approach helps to diminish the "service station" approach that many people—teens and adults—have toward the church where they just show up and expect everything to be done for them.

Admittedly, allowing youth into the planning process makes things a lot messier. They might come up with ideas you aren't too crazy about, and they might fail to follow through. You might even have to give up an idea you love because the teenagers just don't get it. But in the end, you'll have a group that's much more engaged and excited about their ministry. —Brian

At the beginning of my third year of full-time youth ministry, I created a youth leadership team comprised of five high school seniors. I asked them to help me plan the calendar year. We met in June, reviewed all the events and activities of the previous year, and set new goals—both long term and short term—for the upcoming year. For the most part, this process has been helpful in encouraging the youth to take more responsibility for our ministry together.

However, as Brian notes, while teenagers often brainstorm incredible ideas that sound great (and typically need a lot of prep time), they don't always follow through and participate in what they've planned. I've had teens beg me to do a certain activity—for example, visiting a local nursing home. But when it came time to actually go to the nursing home, homework and other commitments such as sports, friends, and life in general suddenly took priority. I've come to see that this is just the nature of working with young people. Inviting them into the planning process helps us to remember that we can't control the whole process. We have to allow room for the unexpected.

Planning for Spontaneity

Whether you have a large ministry or a small one, I still firmly believe that planning the whole year is crucial. However, there should always be space for spontaneity. Flexibility helps us remember that ministry is a communal effort and calling; we don't—and shouldn't—control it. There must be room for teenagers to make plans and change their minds, be inspired by new ideas and shift their priorities. Imagine a night when you've planned for an intense Bible study, but the kids in your group have had a long, stressful week. What they really need, they say, is just an hour or two to rest. Would you be willing to throw out the perfectly planned schedule and simply provide some Sabbath time for the group?

Original Blog Date: October 5

Here's a radical community-builder idea for your youth ministry: Host a night in which you gather together . . . to do nothing!

Okay, maybe not nothing, but pretty close. . . . Announce to your group that your next meeting will be a "Do Nothing Night." You won't be organizing any activities. Invite them to bring their own activities—provided it's something they can do without disturbing others. They could bring board or card games to play with friends. They could bring their journals to write in or their sketchbooks to draw in. They could bring a book to read. Or they could just hang out and talk. Play some quiet music in the background, provide some snacks, and let the group enjoy each other's company. Believe me, most young people have such overloaded schedules that one evening of Sabbath time will be a real gift.

If you just can't resist the urge to program, wrap up the evening with a short time of prayerful worship focused on the spiritual practice of Sabbath rest, perhaps using Exodus 20:8-11 or Deuteronomy 5:12-15. —Brian

True ministry also calls us to be prepared to meet unexpected needs. We have to be flexible enough to deal with the upheavals that life often brings. Brian recalls a church he served while he was in seminary. It was located in a small Illinois steel town. The youth ministry was brand new, and he was tasked with creating it from the ground up. The group included kids from the church and teenagers who'd never set foot in a church. One morning early in the fall, he was preparing for that night's event—a fun outing for the youth group. But as he watched news reports of hijackers crashing commercial airliners into the World Trade Center towers and the Pentagon, he knew the activity had to be scrapped. The group would need that night—and many more—to talk and share their anger, fears, doubts, and questions. They needed to pray together and to sit in silence.

Similarly, when the small country of Haiti was devastated by a 7.0 earthquake in early 2010, we urged the readers of our blog to *drop everything* and make room to talk about this devastating event with their teens.

Original Blog Date: January 14

This weekend, let go of your carefully planned Bible studies, game nights, Wii tournaments, and study programs and just sit with your group and talk about what's happening in Haiti. Print out some of the news photos of the devastation and place them in the center of the group. Give the teens a chance to share what they've heard and read about the crisis. Talk about what your church or denomination is already doing and brainstorm ideas for what your group can do to help. Spend time in group or silent prayer. —Brian

What followed in the post was a list of Bible passages and a series of simple questions to help youth groups talk through the issues that events like these bring up. It was clear from the responses we received to this post that many readers appreciated someone giving them permission to simply drop the planning and go with the moment. One youth leader shared that pushing aside carefully planned programs in order to focus on the Haitian crisis, though important, was not the easiest thing to do. He wrote, "We did this last night at our student service. It's really hard for me to drop something I've been working on for months and replace it with something last minute, but we felt as if it was something God wanted us to do. I took your suggestions and tweaked them a little to fit our students. It was absolutely an amazing night. Both our high school students and our middle school students had some amazing discussions on the event."

Another reader commented, "Thanks again for reminding us that youth ministry is less about what we plan and more about our making room for God to empower us to love and action on behalf of others!"

Planning for ministry means allowing space for real life to happen. You have to be ready to let go of some control so you're free to address those needs for which you simply cannot plan.

For some of us, the idea of letting go of the programming and just being open to the moment can be too much to even consider. Perhaps we fear looking unorganized or less-than-competent in the eyes of church staff or pastors. Maybe we fear negative reactions from parents if things don't go just as we promised. Maybe we're still a little unsure of letting the Spirit move us into uncharted territory. But I've found that it's in that territory that some of the most profound ministry to youth takes place.

I once had a parent tell me the story of how his now-adult daughter had an experience in youth group that deeply influenced her faith development. As a teenager, her attendance in church was limited. She never felt like the youth ministry met her spiritual needs and desires. But something changed one Friday night—the Friday before Easter. At the last minute, the youth leader decided to have a special evening service outdoors. Calls were made. Rides were arranged. Everyone came together. And sitting around a bonfire in the middle of a field, this young lady and her friends experienced the presence of Christ in a deeply spiritual way as they prepared for Easter weekend. If you were to ask what other events she remembers from youth group, the answer would likely be "not many." But that spontaneous experience of worship had a lasting impact.

Getting Started

Whether you plan a whole year at a time or you prefer to be more spontaneous and open-ended, we all have to start somewhere. For many of us, planning starts either with the beginning of the school year or the beginning of the calendar year. I always find the first event of the new season to be full of pressure and expectations. I used to believe that this was the one event where I really wanted to draw in as many youth as possible. I assumed that once I had the teenagers in one place, I could show them everything our church had to offer and convince them they should consider joining us in regular ministry. When it worked, it was fantastic!

Original Blog Date: August 22

Last Sunday night we had our annual Back-to-School Bash. Here are some quick facts from the night: 220 youth in attendance, 75 adult volunteers, 3 local bands, 34 different churches represented, 9 area youth ministers or leaders in the dunking tank, and all together more than 300 people in attendance.

The games were a ton of fun. The music was loud. The food was delicious. But, most importantly, at the conclusion of the evening, when we gathered for worship in the sanctuary, the Spirit of the living God was present and among us all. Every seat in the center of the sanctuary was filled from the front to the back. Youth from 34 different churches joined in prayer, songs, and fellowship. You could feel the energy and sense of community in the air. There was a true sense on Sunday evening that we're all brothers and sisters in Christ. —Jacob

After writing this post, I couldn't help but think of a post Brian had written several weeks earlier. Brian reflected on the significance of beginning your ministry year not with parties and noise, but with opportunities to embrace a spirit of community and contemplation:

Original Blog Date: August 6

Instead of kicking off youth group this fall with a huge, loud, action-filled event designed to attract every teen in town and convince them that "Yes! Church is fun! Church is cool!" what if you thought small? What if you thought quiet? What if you thought restful? What if the first activity that starts off the new school year offered time for youth to break away from the constant noise and activity of their everyday world? What if you created an experience where deep relationship building could begin? What if you set the tone for the whole year by starting off with a mission project focusing outward on the needs of others, rather than inward on the need to be entertained? What if your first gathering modeled contemplation, intentional listening and sharing, and thoughtful prayer, rather than trying to compete with the distractions of popular culture? What if . . . ? —Brian

If you're looking to start your youth ministry year with something less programmed and on a smaller scale, you might consider one of the following ideas:

Plan a mission project. Put the focus on serving others with a group project in your neighborhood or town.

Cook a meal. Join together for a pizza-making night (or some other simple meal) that will give your group a chance to develop community, talk, laugh, cooperate, and break bread together. Turn the meal into a sacred love feast celebration of Communion.

Create group art. If done as a group, creative art projects can be fun for artists and non-artists alike because the focus is on the collaborative process, rather than the end result. Paint a mural together, build a sculpture, craft prayer flags, make masks, or create a group portrait.

Make tie-dyed T-shirts. This is a fun, messy project that anyone can do. You'll end up with cool, hand-designed shirts.

Build community. Lead some noncompetitive team-building activities to illustrate the way the body of Christ works together. These sorts of games take the focus off winning or losing and encourage a sense of unity in the group.

Practice Sabbath. Unless you want to send the message that every gathering will be a high-octane activity, why not plan an afternoon or evening of rest, silence, and creative contemplation?

Lead a worship experience. Divide into teams and plan a collaborative worship service. End the evening by bringing together all the gifts of the group.

Finding the Balance

Ultimately I believe there needs to be a healthy balance between events like the Back-to-School Bash and quieter times of service and spiritual reflection. Somehow there has to be a balance between events that facilitate large group experiences and events that provide opportunities for quiet reflection and spiritual growth.

I've known youth ministers who create impressive, elaborate spreadsheets of what their youth will do and learn for every year they're in church. Each Sunday's teachings and activities—for both Christian education classes and youth group—are planned in precise detail. I admit that at times I'm jealous of this level of organization. By the time a young woman graduates from one of these churches, her youth leader is able to tell you exactly what concepts, ideas, and Scripture passages she learned and at what age.

On the other hand, this approach is almost too controlling. It leaves little room for young people to help shape the ministry, and it tends to treat faith as something that can be packaged and dispensed at regular intervals. I just don't believe the Christian life is this predictable. If we're serious about helping teenagers follow the way of Jesus, perhaps some of our planning should reflect the radical—and at times surprising—ministry that Jesus practiced and preached.

Original Blog Date: December 30

As we get ready for a new year, I can't help but think about this year and what I would have changed or done differently. Overall I think the year has been a success. But there are always opportunities to grow and become more creative. Here are a few ideas I'm thinking of for next year.

- Prayer: This seems obvious, but so many of the events we plan for—from retreats to ice skating—aren't rooted in prayer. Perhaps during the beginning stages of planning, we should pray for discernment in our youth ministry. This year I hope to have a prayer ministry team, composed of a variety of ages, who will pray weekly (maybe prior to each youth meeting) for our ministry to young people and for the church as a whole.

- Monasticism: What? Hear me out. Lately I've been really drawn to the ancient monastics and how their lives were rooted in prayer and work. The young people I work with are drawn to radical lifestyles. When I talk about the ascetic lifestyles of the monastics and the powerful challenges posed to both themselves and others in terms of fasting, prayer, and worship, my teens often want to learn more and experience something similar (albeit not as extreme). What if you were to plan for Desert Days with your youth? Plan for a day, perhaps once a month, where you and your group spend an entire day isolated from everyone else—no cell phones, computers, or video games.

- Mission: At our youth group meetings, we spend a lot of time talking about ways to reach out to others. But what if we really put our ideas into action? For example, in the days leading up to Thanksgiving, talk about what it means to share a meal together and how Jesus invited complete strangers to a wonderful banquet. Then do the same. Prepare a meal at your church, set the table, and then go out and invite strangers to share a meal with you. I guarantee this is an event your youth will remember for the rest of their lives.

- Worship: Encourage your young people to participate more fully in the life of the church. Have teenagers read Scripture, lead prayers, and even preach. We learn what it means to worship through both observation and participation.

- Leadership: This is an area in which I really need to spend more time planning and empowering. Encourage your teenagers to be leaders not only in youth group,

but also in the overall life of the church. Consider having teens serve on the church board—not as youth representatives, but as fully functioning board members.
—Jacob

Of course this is just a sampling of creative approaches to planning for your youth ministry. To know what's right for your teens and your church, gather together a small group of people who can help you rethink what you're doing and why.

Take the time to evaluate the ministry and what you're trying to accomplish together. Does your planning allow for creativity? Are you challenged to move beyond your comfort zone? Do you allow for spontaneity and flexibility? Once you have a clear sense of what you want to offer teens and what you hope to accomplish, start brainstorming ways to get there. Take the time to be creative, find what works for you, let go of the stranglehold of planned programming, and start living out your ministry together.

Brian's Reflections

Back when I was a public school teacher, organization was a must. I wouldn't have survived my first semester if I hadn't learned to plan ahead and have a sense of where I was leading my teens. Youth ministry is no different, though I have to believe that failure to plan in youth ministry will have far greater consequences than failing to teach long division.

Youth ministry is a sacred calling and it demands our excellence. Without careful planning, even our best intentions won't provide the young people in our care with the spiritual direction they need and deserve. I appreciate Jacob's honest recounting of his first year of ministry, and I can certainly relate to the obstacles we youth workers face when we fail to plan. I agree that creating a long-range plan for one year of ministry is helpful and that developing a plan that covers all the years a teen might be in your ministry may be helpful as well.

But rather than filling up a spreadsheet with specific Scriptures to be memorized, we need to think about broader goals such as:

- What experiences with the gospel do we want our young people to have during their time in our ministry?
- Which church leadership roles do we need to help our youth try on for size during their time in middle and high school?
- What opportunities for hands-on ministry—both inside and outside the church—do we need to plan for over the course of the total youth ministry program for each teen?

Note that the most important word in all of those questions is *we*. This sort of long-range planning, as Jacob has suggested, should be done with the community of faith. Invite parents, church leaders, and youth into the conversation so the entire community has ownership of your long-range plans.

Jacob also mentions the inherent frustrations when planning with young people. It's worth remembering that in Scripture God often called the most unlikely people to be leaders—including youth. Some succeeded and some failed, but always God supported and encouraged them to be the people they were created to be. We owe no less to the youth in our care as they explore the ministries in the church that call to their hearts.

Inevitably even young people with the best of intentions will fail to follow through, or will plan an event but not show up to lead it, or will get the group excited about an idea and then lose interest. Although involving young people in the planning of their ministry is a must, we shouldn't burden them with the full weight of organizing and leading the programming. Allow the adults in your ministry to act as guides and mentors so the youth feel free to experiment, brainstorm, dream, and even experience failure—all while knowing that caring adults are there to help them along the way.

Rethinking Your Own Ministry

- How are you planning your youth ministry? What are your short- and long-term goals? Consider taking the time to write out your goals and evaluate them with others who are involved in your ministry.

- In what ways might you be overplanning your ministry?

- Are you planning for a program or for ministry? Do you agree there's a difference?

- Meet with a small group of teenagers from your church. Ask them to help you evaluate the youth ministry. What activities and elements of the ministry do they find beneficial? What would they change?

- How are you intentionally engaging others in the planning? Do you have both adults and teenagers working together to envision the future?

chapter 6

why you don't need volunteers

Jacob

I'll never forget the night I learned a priceless lesson about the role of adult participation in youth ministry. It was January and I'd been lucky enough to have a wonderful group of adults working with me since the beginning of the school year. They were well prepared, enthusiastic about working with teenagers, and beginning to form relationships with some of the kids.

One night after youth group, one of our teens came up to me and asked, "What are these adults doing here?"

I said, "What do you mean? They've been coming to youth group since September. They help us out."

"They do?" she replied with a rather skeptical look on her face. "I've never seen them before. Are you sure?"

That's when I realized I'd made a mistake. I tried to recall how I'd introduced these volunteers at the start of the school year. But I couldn't remember because I hadn't done it. I'd just assumed that because the adults were doing all the things I needed them to do, their role was obvious to the teenagers. I'd never truly integrated them into our ministry, and that had been detrimental for all of us.

It had short-changed the teens because they'd lost out on months of potential connection with adults who truly cared about them. It was unfair to my volunteers because it prevented them from having a real sense of involvement in the mission of our ministry. And it had put me in a position that I didn't really want to be in, one where—in the eyes of the youth, at least—I was the only one in charge.

A youth ministry is only as strong as the adults who are a part of it. The challenge for a youth minister is to find other adults who share a passion for young people and will commit to building a missional youth ministry.

The Call of a Congregation

Brian and I have both served congregations who just assumed that the youth minister and youth ministry team took care of the teens. Translation: You do it so we don't have to. Yet in most churches when a young person is baptized, we vow as a community of faith to work together to walk with that child on his or her spiritual journey. Taking an interest in teenagers is part of that vow.

Original Blog Date: January 25

Each year our church has both dedications for babies and baptisms for teenagers. Over time I've started to view these events as rites of passage—both for the participant and the congregation. The congregation is asked if they will help raise this child and guide her in the Christian faith. Such questions take seriously the notion that as communities of faith, we're all required to help raise disciples of Christ.

But all too often it's a small group of individuals who work with our children and youth. For the past several weeks, I've been thinking about how we can change that.

What if we no longer had volunteers but instead focused on spiritual mentors? Spiritual mentors—people of all ages and spectrums of life—could be with our youth through all the years they're growing up in church. What would it look like to have spiritual mentors—people who are intentional about par-

ticipating in the entire spiritual formation and Christian education of our young people? —Jacob

How would your church respond if you put an article in the church newsletter with the headline: "Volunteers No Longer Needed"? Imagine if we dropped the word *volunteers* and with it the implication that caring for the youth of the church is just a choice made by a few. Instead, through our process of discernment, we could call adults into youth ministry to serve as spiritual mentors who would—

- Be present at rites of passage for teenagers in the church.
- Pray for our young people on a regular basis.
- Offer pastoral care to teenagers in times of anxiety and challenge.
- Accompany and be regularly present for mission trips, summer camps, and retreats.
- Learn alongside young people in Sunday school or youth group.
- Set an example for young people in the way they live, worship, play, and interact with others.

For some, these expectations would be too much. But for others, this serious and thoughtful approach to inviting adult participation could help them see how vital youth ministry is. Try encouraging spiritual mentorship and you'll be surprised by who says, "Yes. Sign me up!"

If you're lucky, you'll find adults who will build on your strengths as a leader and make up for your weaknesses. If you're not into organization, find someone who is. Not into sports? Find someone who's uniquely gifted to help teens in this area. Are you great at the details but sometimes miss the big picture? Seek out those who can help cast a vision for your ministry.

This is more than putting new words to an old idea. It's what I missed when I neglected to introduce those adult volunteers to my youth group. I hadn't thought of them as being a part of the spiritual formation of the teens in the group. They were my assistants, my helpers. But when we see these gracious adults as partners and participants in the lives of teenagers, their role becomes so crucial that we could never mistake them for mere chaperones.

Thinking in terms of spiritual mentorship changes everything about how we find and encourage adult volunteers—how we invite them, what we expect of them, and how we integrate them into our groups. All of that starts with prayer.

A Process of Prayer and Discernment

Five years ago, right before I started working at my current church, the youth ministry was led almost entirely by adult volunteers. Over time there's been a gradual shift in responsibilities and accountability so that almost all of the day-to-day functions of youth ministry fall to me and our coordinator of youth ministry. We still have some tremendous volunteers, but we've shifted away from the emphasis on volunteers that was once the hallmark of this church. In many ways that's been good for our community, but I'm not sure it's the best arrangement.

Last fall we decided to rethink our approach to using volunteers.

Original Blog Date: July 15

As we begin to plan for the upcoming school year, it occurs to me how important it is to have committed adult volunteers and leaders. Somehow there needs to be a balance between staff-driven and lay-driven ministry. The advantage to staff-driven ministry is that you're able to control how and when events unfold. The disadvantage arises out of the same scenario—YOU are overseeing events. Whenever youth ministry begins to focus more on staff and less on volunteers, I think there's a need to reflect on how ministry is taking place. Everyone leads such hectic and busy lives (this is another topic in itself). But what can we do to purposefully engage our adult volunteers and leaders? —Jacob

Since writing those thoughts, I've come to believe that the first step in finding volunteers in youth ministry should be a serious process of prayer and discernment. All too often I've been guilty of the opposite approach—calling everyone I can think of and asking them to fill in at the last minute because nobody else is available. You know how the conversation goes: "We really need your help this fall. There's just no one else available to help teach Sunday school. If we can't find somebody, we're going to have to combine some of the classes." While I'd never say it out loud, I know I was trying to guilt somebody into being a teacher. I was hoping they'd serve out of a sense of obligation—especially if their child was involved with the youth ministry.

How often do we recruit adult leaders in youth ministry for all the wrong reasons?

- He answered the open plea in the church newsletter.
- There was no one else available.
- She has lots of time on her hands and was willing to do it.
- We just need a warm body to help chaperone.

Maybe we convince ourselves that any adult will do in a pinch. Or perhaps we believe that deep down we can do it all and the other adults are just there to support us. Or maybe we're desperate for a little help and are willing to take the first person who walks through the door. We've all been there.

But I've started to realize just how ineffective—and ultimately harmful—such recruitment tactics can be to a ministry. Recruiting help on short notice often leads to volunteers who, though well meaning, are unsuited for the task, overwhelmed by expectations, or destined to lose interest quickly. But we aren't just looking for helpers. We're looking for mentors.

There is a better way. It starts with an ongoing process of discernment. Well before a new season of youth group begins, start praying and reflecting on who would be a good fit for your ministry. And as you reflect, consider the goals and vision of your ministry. What do the young people in your group need—the wisdom of more mature Christians? The liveliness of college students? The thoughtfulness of parents? Also consider what you know about the congregation. What spiritual gifts do you see in the people? Talk to other adults in the church to find out who they think might be gifted for ministry to young people. And talk to your youth group. Who would they like to invite into their lives?

This process, though certainly more complicated than grabbing the first people who raise their hands to volunteer, acknowledges that there are some people in your congregation who are particularly gifted for ministry with youth. Taking the time to figure out who they are shows respect both for their unique calling of ministry and for the level of care you expect for the teenagers you serve.

Taking the time to go through a discernment process also allows you to tell potential mentors, "We've been prayerfully considering this. We believe you have unique gifts for ministry with young people, and we ask that before you give us an answer, you spend some time in prayer, too." Once I started using this process of discernment, I found that the volunteers who joined us had a stronger connection to the ministries that were taking place. They understood they weren't just serving as a warm body or as a chaperone. They were being called into ministry.

Offer a Test Run

Oftentimes in our quest for volunteers, we forget that many adults think of teenagers as wild, crazy, unruly, and disrepectful. There is some truth to this, of course. But for the most part, being in ministry with youth is extremely rewarding. Teenagers are honest, up-front, and excited about their relationship with God.

In order to show adults just how fulfilling youth ministry can be, consider inviting potential volunteers to sit in on a Sunday school class or youth group gathering without the pressure of feeling as though they are there to lead an activity or make a solid commitment to volunteering. If they're willing, ask the adults to share a bit of their faith story with the group. Even if they decide that volunteering in youth ministry isn't for them, they'll have made a connection with the young people at the church.

For two summers we centered our Sunday school class for grades 6 through 12 around conversational and relaxed gatherings with different adults from the church. Sunday mornings would start with the teens just hanging out, eating donuts, and chatting with one another. Then an adult from the congregation would join us to share his faith story. We invited a variety of adults to do this—younger, older, new members, old members, doctors, stay-at-home parents, teachers, and farmers—basically anyone who was willing to talk about her life in Christ. And we made a point of inviting people our teenagers didn't already know. The goal was to form relationships around the sharing of story.

After the adult finished speaking, we broke off into groups. The teenagers spent the next 15 minutes reflecting on what they'd heard and brainstorming a list of questions to ask the presenter. Then we wrapped up our time with these visitors with a Q&A session.

By inviting people who weren't traditionally a part of youth group events and activities, we were able to break through some of the adults' assumptions and stereotypes about teenagers. And that dramatically enlarged our pool of people who might be interested in volunteering. We also helped form relationships between the youth and a wide range of adults in the church—and that's a kind of spiritual mentorship, too.

Don't be afraid to think outside the box. Despite what most churches seem to think, to be a great youth volunteer you don't have to be a 20-something male with a goatee, slim waist, and proficiency in 10 sports. When seeking spiritual mentors for your teens, help your youth experience the diversity in your church. Senior citizens can be great with youth! Married couples and single people each bring a unique perspective. A college or graduate student can add a whole new dimension to your team.

What about Parents?

An obvious way to add depth to your volunteer list is to involve the parents. Of course this can be treacherous territory since the last thing many teenagers want is to have their parents hanging around when they're with their friends. But we can't overlook the important influence that parents can and should have on the faith formation of their children—they are the ultimate spiritual mentors.

We can teach all the Bible studies we want, but ultimately the parents have the most important and lasting influence on a young person's faith—for good or ill. Sometimes using a few parents as regular volunteers can be a powerful asset to a ministry, just as long as we follow the same process of discernment that we use to consider other adults—including asking their teens for permission first!

But there are other ways to connect parents with our ministries. We've found great success in putting together a parents' small group that meets at the same time as our youth group. The parents enjoy this time to connect, pray, and offer each other support. And because they're already in the building, the parents are available to help with events and activities if we're short-handed or if something seems too great to miss.

I've also discovered a fringe benefit to this group: It helps with attendance. For years we had sporadic attendance in our youth group. We always had a decent number of teens attending, but never the same group of kids each week. It was hard to build a sense of community and shared mission when the dynamics of the group kept changing. Once our parents' group started meeting at the same time as the youth group, attendance stabilized. If parents are at church, it's almost guaranteed that their teenagers will be there, too.

Top 10 Things Every Adult Should Know about Teens

Once your teens' spiritual mentors hear the call, we need to ensure they're provided with the training and resources they need to succeed. But remember, most of what they need they most likely already possess. We aren't calling them to lead programs but to be a presence in the lives of teenagers.

Still, it doesn't hurt to help adults remember a little bit about what it's like to be a teenager. A few years ago our youth ministry team put together a Top 10 list of things adults should know about teens. It's just for fun, but it definitely holds some truth as well.

1. Teens are people, too. Resist calling them *kids* (unless you mean it as a term of endearment) or talking about them as if they aren't in the room.

2. Teens need time. It takes teenagers some time to think about what they want to say, particularly during discussions. Resist the temptation to jump in with the *right* answer and don't feel you have to fill every moment of silence with talking.

3. Teens like adults. Despite what you may remember from your younger days, teens do enjoy the companionship of adults. They just aren't always sure if we like them back, so they can seem standoffish at times. The truth is many teenagers are at a point in their lives when they're trying to put a little distance between themselves and their parents. So they often seek other caring adults to serve as mentors and role models.

4. Teens have a lot to teach us. In many ways that '80s film *The Breakfast Club* got it right: Young people are unique individuals with unique talents, gifts, attitudes, and perspectives. It would be a mistake to lump them all together as one homogenous group.

5. Teens' body clocks are different than ours. Most teens need 8 to 10 hours of sleep a night, yet they often get much less than that. Most teens aren't at their peak until late morning, and many of them are night owls. That means they have a ton of energy in the evenings and can be hyped up just when you're settling down. Keep in mind that they aren't being hyper to bug you. They're just experiencing the high point of their day.

6. Teens are passionate. The first part of the teenage brain to fully develop is the emotional center. That means teens can have high highs and low lows all in one day. They're sensitive to the pain of others and can be very passionate about the things they believe in.

7. Teens want to own their experiences. When teens talk about their struggles, we adults are tempted to say things like, "Oh, I went through the same thing at your age," or "I had the same problems and I survived just fine," or "Here's how I handled that problem." In many ways the experiences of teens today are quite different from when we were young. Their struggles are real and they want them to be taken seriously, not dismissed with an "I survived that and you will, too." Oftentimes the best approach with young people isn't offering advice but just listening.

8. Teens are fun to be around. Adults may think that hanging with adolescents will make them feel old, but it's just the opposite. Teens offer a perspective on life and the world that's refreshingly honest, hopeful, and new. That sense of hope and possibility can be contagious.

9. Teens can be a great source of frustration. Yes, teenagers are great. But let's be realistic: They can be incredibly frustrating to work with . . . unless you are willing to be flexible, can take a little good-natured ribbing and criticism (have I mentioned the girl who always tells me when my tie doesn't match my suit?), and remember that they still have a lot of growing up to do. This leads to the final item on this list.

10. Teens are not adults. No matter how much they might look or act like adults, teens are still children—in the best sense of the word. For every moment of maturity, they have other moments in which they grumble about taking out the trash, neglect their responsibilities, fight with their best friends (and then make up with them an hour later), and choose goofing off over doing their work. Don't expect them to act like adults. Expect them to act like young people who are still growing, adjusting, stumbling, and trying to figure it all out.

Making Connections

Once your adult mentors are in place and are comfortable with the goals of your ministry, help them discover meaningful ways to connect with young people. Here are a few suggestions to help build the kind of relationships that facilitate spiritual mentorship:

Get rid of the curriculum. Our task is to mentor teens not teach lessons. Teenagers go to school five days a week and don't need one more day of school on Sundays. So stop focusing on getting through the prescribed lesson plans and focus on the individuals instead. Give yourself permission to occasionally set aside the workbooks and worksheets and allow your *curriculum* to grow organically from current issues and themes that are important to your teenagers. Tie Bible studies to newspaper articles, current movies, TV shows, stories, or problems your teens are facing in their daily lives. Generate a list of moral, ethical, and what-if questions and get your youth talking. Out of these discussions, you'll get all sorts of clues as to what they need most in terms of theological guidance.

Create a relaxed setting. No more sitting around tables or in rows of chairs facing a speaker or teacher at the front of the room. Set up your youth room—or any other space in the church—with comfortable seating arranged in a circle. I'm not advocating the notion of a youth room crammed with distractions like video games and loud music. Rather, create a comfortable space where teenagers feel free to share and talk.

Get out of the building. Christian education and relationship formation with spiritual mentors don't have to take place inside the church. Why not make use of a nearby coffeehouse or donut shop, a park, or the church lawn? Just remember to follow the adult-teen relationship boundary guidelines we addressed in chapter 4.

Make it intergenerational. Youth ministry is moving away from a teen-centered model to a church-centered model. It's time we stop isolating teens from the wider church fellowship. As a church look for ways to connect the generations. How about semi-regular Sunday morning forums focused on issues of social justice, culture, and theology for all ages? Both adults and teenagers can learn so much just from listening to one another talk about these issues.

Practice spiritual disciplines. Just like anything else, spiritual disciplines take practice. Consider offering weekly opportunities for teenagers and their spiritual mentors to experience prayer stations together or try *Lectio Divina* or simply observe the Sabbath through restful times of casual conversation and quiet reflection.

Create short-term experiences. Keep young people and their spiritual mentors interested by regularly reforming the Sunday morning and evening youth group experience. You might spend time in the fall focused on planning and carrying out mission projects. During Advent turn the group into a drama team and prepare a series of skits to augment the worship services. In the winter you could transform the group time into a film series and tie your discussion to movies selected by the teens. When spring rolls around, study other faiths and denominations and arrange visits to other churches and places of worship. In the summer months, you can morph into a photography club by inviting teens and their spiritual mentors to create a group slideshow using the images of God that they find in the neighborhood around the church or throughout your city. And be sure to ask your young people and adult mentors for their ideas as well. In this way you'll have no problem filling up the year with meaningful events and opportunities for growth and connection.

How Are We Doing?

Volunteers and spiritual mentors also need to be equipped with the tools to evaluate, from a spiritual perspective, their role in the ministry and how well they're working together. One excellent approach is to encourage your spiritual mentors to use the Awareness Examen.

Original Blog Date: September 26

The Awareness Examen is an ancient prayer practice that invites reflection on the day—the ways in which God was present to you and how you responded to that presence. This particular prayer practice was developed by Ignatius of Loyola as a daily discipline of reflection on God's activity in our lives. I use a form of this prayer following each youth group event or meeting as a way to avoid the trap of always reflecting on just the positives or just the negatives of a particular gathering. If a Bible study goes particularly well, it's easy to pat ourselves on the back and take all the credit for what talented youth leaders we are. If the youth group meeting bombs, it's just as easy to beat ourselves up about it all the way home and wonder if it's time to find a real job!

Use of the Awareness Examen invites more thoughtful reflection on our ministry and the movement of God's Spirit. Here's how you can use this prayer practice for yourself and your leaders:

- Find a quiet place and take some time to center yourself.
- Think back over the meeting or event or gathering as if you were watching a movie of all that happened. What did you notice? What feelings or thoughts do you associate with the meeting?
- Think about where you saw God at work during the time together. Give thanks for these moments.
- Think about times during the meeting when you or others might have been unaware of God's presence.
- Think about times during the meeting when you or others might have been resisting God's presence. Ask for forgiveness for this shortsightedness.
- Consider where God might be calling you to a new awareness. What new places might God be calling you to in your ministry?
- Give thanks for the time together with your group and for God's presence within each person there. —Brian

Celebrating Your Adult Leaders

Lastly, and most importantly, find ways to honor and affirm the ministry of your spiritual mentors.

- Send postcards thanking them for all of their time and leadership.
- Introduce the leaders of your youth ministry to the entire church.
- Host a special Sunday where you lift up all of the different ways that lay leaders make the youth ministry possible.
- Give them small gifts during the holidays (Thanksgiving, Christmas, Valentine's Day) to thank them for all they do.
- Invite all of your mentors to your house for brunch.
- Encourage your teens to write letters to their spiritual mentors that talk about what the relationship means to them.

Be creative and attentive to the needs, concerns, and joys of your adult leaders. If those you serve with know that you care about them and appreciate their efforts, they'll make your entire ministry stronger.

Brian's Reflections

Wow! All of these years I've been saying "volunteers" when I should have been saying "spiritual mentors." Actually, I couldn't agree more. I've worked with a lot of lay youth leaders over the years, and some were clearly called to the ministry and some were not. Those who are called seemed to stick with it no matter what. They showed up to youth events without fail. They sat with teenagers during worship. They slept on hard church floors at every lock-in. They took a week off of work every summer to go to camp or on a mission trip. Most importantly they enjoyed the company of teenagers and genuinely cared about helping them learn and grow.

How can you tell the difference between an adult who's just biding her time in your program and the one who's really called to youth ministry? Simple: Check in with her in a few years and see if she's still in youth ministry. The ones who are truly called to work with youth can't help but keep doing it—in spite of the challenges.

Jacob suggests that we not limit our ideas about the kinds of adults who might be called to ministry with youth. But since our task here is to build missional ministries, I'd like to throw out one caveat for consideration when choosing adult leaders: age.

I've read youth ministry blogs that suggest that once you turn 40, you're probably too old to be working with teens; and at age 50 you're definitely too old! I couldn't disagree more. In fact I imagine many of our ministries would greatly benefit from a few more seasoned adults with amazing life experiences to share, not to mention a longer faith journey.

For many reasons young adults lead a great number of youth ministries today. I myself began leading a youth group at age 23, so I'm not casting doubt that those who are in their 20s can be called to ministry with youth. I fully believe I was called to youth ministry at that early age, but I certainly had a great deal to learn. I was still trying to figure out who I was, let alone serve as an expert on helping teens navigate the ups and downs of adolescence.

Fortunately, I was blessed in those early years with pastors and older adult youth leaders who helped serve as my mentors. I would encourage anyone who enters youth ministry leadership at an early age, whether as a pastor or volunteer, to surround themselves with older, more mature Christians who can provide plenty of supervision and help develop and maintain boundaries.

Thankfully I also felt drawn to become a teacher in those early years of youth ministry, and much of what I experienced as a professional educator forced me to be a better minister to youth. Now in my 40s, I finally feel like I have some sort of handle on what I'm doing. I have more patience and more perspective but just as much idealism. And I expect to be even better when I'm 50!

There are plenty of advantages to being a young youth minister. And there are plenty of advantages to being an old youth minister. What would it be like if every church teamed the two together? Ultimately, I'm inclined to say that the real issue is less the age of the person and more his or her motivation for wanting to serve in youth ministry. We owe it to both our ministries and our potential leaders to thoughtfully and faithfully engage in the sort of process of discernment that Jacob suggests. Most importantly, we owe it to our teens.

Rethinking Your Own Ministry

- How do you currently call someone into youth ministry? What changes might be needed in your approach?

- How does your ministry train spiritual mentors?

- What qualities of adult leadership does your ministry need right now?

- What role do your youth play in finding leaders for your ministry?

- Are you intentional about seeking out intergenerational volunteers? If not, what might be holding you back?

- Which potential youth leaders might you be overlooking in your congregation because they don't fit the typical youth leader mold?

chapter 7

the end of
educational
ministry

Brian

In the Gospel of Matthew, we encounter Jesus' parable about a hidden treasure (Matthew 13:44). A plowman is working out in the field, doing what plowmen do, when he stumbles upon a treasure left behind by someone else. Now, what does this plowman do? Does he grab the treasure and run? Does he cover it up and make a map so he can sneak back under the cover of night and spirit the treasure away? Well, almost. He does cover up the treasure, but then, surprisingly, he goes and sells all that he has and buys the field! What sense does this make? He had the treasure. Why not simply spirit it away?

As with each of Jesus' parables, the true meaning of the story can come as a surprise: The treasure isn't worth having if it belongs to someone else. The plowman wants to make it his own.

Original Blog Date: January 12

There was a time when I subscribed to the idea that Christian education was kind of like putting a funnel into someone's head and pouring in knowledge. *What do teenagers need to know? I'd ask myself. The books of the Bible? The major biblical characters? The teachings of Jesus? The dogma of the church? The Trinity? The church seasons?* And on and on I'd go. It was exhausting trying to figure out how to cram all of that information (and more) into my teens' heads during the few short years that I had them under my influence.

But gradually a new metaphor for Christian education began taking shape in my thinking—that of fellow travelers. In this understanding, youth pastors become less like teachers and more like spiritual companions accompanying young people on their journey of faith, so we don't so much lead as walk beside. —Brian

The parable of the plowman is a good reminder that faith isn't handed to us. It's something we happen upon and make our own. For those of us who are blessed to serve in ministry with youth, one of our primary callings is to provide young people with the spiritual tools and guidance they need to make a faith journey of their own. Essentially we must teach them how to acquire their own fields so they feel a sense of ownership for the treasures of their faith.

Now this all sounds very well and good, but too often in the church we take the opposite approach. We expect teenagers to stand on the side of the field and watch us dig for treasure. We expect them to receive the treasure we've already uncovered. Setting aside the metaphor for a moment, youth workers have a bad habit of telling teenagers what to think—about the Bible, the church, Jesus, God, abortion, sexuality, the faith journey—rather than letting them seek the answers for themselves within a Christian community.

I'll be the first to admit that presenting teenagers with Christian belief in a beribboned box is fairly easy to do. There's comfort in believing our teens are willing to accept ideas about faith that we've already found to be true (that treasure that we dug out of the field long ago). In short it's easier to tell teens what to think (and what not to think) than to walk with them through the long and sometimes difficult process of discovery—especially if we believe we've already found the right answers. The problem is that the brain doesn't learn that way. And even if it *did*, would this approach really constitute authentic faith formation?

Perhaps the toughest lesson I experienced during my years as a schoolteacher was this: You cannot *make* the brain learn anything. I could spend all day at the chalkboard teaching long division, but that didn't necessarily translate to my kids magically being able to divide 112 into 552. Teaching isn't as simple as opening the top of the head and dropping in knowledge. Yet oftentimes this is the very approach we take in youth ministry. When we drill memory verses from Scripture, when we preach dogma, when we tell teenagers what to think about this Bible story or that theological concept, we're attempting to force feed their brains. That's definitely the approach I took in my early days in youth ministry. Had you quizzed my youth group from one Sunday to the next, they might remember some of what I'd taught the previous week. But the truth is that the faith they parroted back to me was really mine, not theirs. Now I know there's a far better way.

One of my favorite passages of Scripture is the story of the road to Emmaus (Luke 24:13-35). It's perhaps the best biblical example of how we might rethink our approach to teaching and learning in youth ministry. Two disciples (likely a man and woman) are wandering down a dirt road, headed for the town of Emmaus. Distraught and somber following Jesus' crucifixion, they encounter a stranger on the road. Of course we know this person to be the risen Christ, but the disciples don't recognize him. So they begin telling this stranger about the amazing recent events in Jerusalem.

What I love about this story are all the things Jesus doesn't do. He doesn't step in as the expert. He doesn't jump in and give them the answers to their distress and worry. He doesn't even reveal himself. He simply walks with them, talks with them, and goes with them on their journey. It's only later, while they're eating together, that these disciples come to realize that Christ has been in their midst. And once they realize that, their entire perspective changes.

This journey to Emmaus can guide our approach to teaching in youth ministry. Rather than seeing ourselves as handing our teenagers a prepackaged faith, we must become their fellow travelers and companions for the journey.

There are several advantages to viewing ourselves as spiritual companions rather than transmitters of dogma. As companions much of the weight is taken off our shoulders. We no longer have to pretend to be experts on the Bible and Christian theology, history, and tradition. We no longer have to know all the answers or pretend we have a rock-solid faith.

But this journey has its difficulties, too. We must give up a lot of power and control over the learning process. Walking alongside youth, rather than running out in front of them, means that sometimes we'll let them determine the direction of the journey. And sometimes we'll discover they have something to teach us.

Given all of this, we might ask: *If we're just fellow travelers, do we have any responsibility at all as educators of youth?* My answer is an emphatic *yes!* In this new role as companion, our call is to help teenagers deepen their journey of faith. We can do that by helping them make connections between their old learning and the new insights you discover together, creating experiences where they can explore God's world and call on their lives, and encouraging them to reflect on these new connections and experiences as a way to more fully understand their place in the kingdom of God.

Teaching to Make Connections

It's the nightmare of every youth worker. You've spent all week planning a lesson that you're confident will engage your youth group. The talk you've written is eloquent, includes just the right number of jokes and stories, and seems relevant to the lives of teens. The follow-up questions are crafted perfectly to allow the group to demonstrate that they've learned the crucial bullet points of your message. The room is precisely arranged to encourage everyone to focus on your words and be enthralled by your wisdom.

Then along comes Wednesday night and . . . it's a disaster. Rather than being engaged, the youth just sit there. No one is willing to answer a question. No one seems even the slightest bit interested in anything you have to say. It's not like you haven't seen this reaction before: the glazed eyes, the slumped-in-the-seat posture, the long yawn, the vacant gaze out the window. We've all been there and it can be disheartening. We had the best of intentions. We transmitted the information. Why didn't the lesson work?

Take a little trip back in time with me for a moment. The youth group I attended when I was a teenager took a very traditional approach to learning. Our meeting room was set up lecture-style with rows of chairs all facing forward so we could give our full attention to whichever adult was offering the program. There was some give-and-take with the speaker, but we never said much. And that was okay with us. We knew that if we sat and listened politely, the torture would end more quickly and we could get on with the games and the food.

Thinking back now, I can't recall one single scrap of information or insight that I received from those programs, though I'm certain some were quite thoughtful. I can't even remember any of the topics—except one. In a change from the normal scheme of things, my youth director invited me to lead a discussion on a topic of my choosing. As you can imagine, I put a great deal of time into preparing that program. Even today, some 25 years later, I can remember what I taught, how I taught it, and what I was hoping my fellow teens would learn.

Of all the Bible studies and discussions I sat through during my years in youth group, why is *that* the only one that sticks in my brain? I think the answer is pretty obvious. By allowing me to prepare the lesson, teach the content, and engage my peers, my youth leader was inviting me to make connections between what I already understood about my faith and how I saw the world as a teenager.

What made this learning experience different from all the others that failed to capture my interest was something I call *the hook*. Put simply, in order for the brain to learn, we often need a hook—a way to help the brain grab on to the learning, make sense of this new information, and relate it to what we already know, feel, and believe to be true about the world. In short, *the hook* is all about helping the brain make a connection.

Comprised of billions of neurons, our brains are really quite adaptable. The brain is continually making new connections as neurons talk to each other via chemicals in the brain. In fact we might say the brain *craves* connections and is constantly working to gather neurons into networks or neuronal branches. Simultaneously the brain takes a sort of use-it-or-lose-it approach, pruning the branches that aren't needed or used regularly. (This explains why you don't remember much from your high school calculus class!)

One important question the brain asks during this networking and pruning process is, *Does this new knowledge connect to my previous learning?* The brain wants to figure out how to connect the new to the old. This is where we can be either a help or a hindrance in the spiritual formation of our young people.

Let's say I plan to introduce a youth group study on the character of God. A big topic to be sure, but I decide to have the group jump into it feetfirst by looking at the book of Isaiah. I begin the lesson by assigning different verses to pairs of teens, telling them to study the verses together and be prepared to share their findings on what Isaiah says about God.

The first thing I notice is that many of the teams are talking about all sorts of fascinating things, but most of their conversations have nothing to do with the texts in Isaiah. When the time comes to share, I discover that while some have gleaned a nugget or two of understanding from the Scripture, most seem disconnected and uninterested. It's clear they're just counting the minutes until snack time.

What went wrong here? Why did the study fail to engage the group? Maybe looking at a different approach to this study will help answer those questions.

Original Blog Date: February 14

Not too long ago, I wrote about a study that discussed the prevalence in our culture of people thinking of God as a sort of cosmic do-gooder. This God keeps his distance, except when you want something from him. This God's foremost concern is our happiness, but beyond that we don't have much need for him. I'm glad to report that this past Sunday my youth group demonstrated that they have a much more nuanced understanding of God than that.

We began the evening by inviting the young people to go out into the church building and find some object or artifact that might symbolize or represent some part of their understanding of God. The results were as varied and diverse as the teens in the group. Some of the objects they shared included—

- A plant, to represent the way we experience God in nature
- A microphone, to show the way God speaks through our lives
- A portrait of Jesus, to show God's coming to earth through his Son
- A toy hen, to symbolize God as Creator
- An offering plate, to symbolize God as the One who gives
- A chair, to represent God's support for us
- The game of *Operation*, to symbolize God as healer

It was only later in the discussion, after everyone had talked about their current understanding of God, that we stopped to look at a series of Scripture texts to consider how our ancient spiritual ancestors symbolized their experience of God. As we read through each passage, the teens wrote on a large sheet of paper those words or images that they felt reflected the way God's nature was described by the author of the text. —Brian

I hope the difference between these two approaches is clear. In the first example, the activity is really teacher-focused. No attempt was made to take into account previous learning of the youth (those neuronal networks I mentioned earlier). We just jumped into the lesson with no sense of what knowledge or understanding the teens already possessed. This approach ignores the fact that teenagers come to us with their heads already full of ideas they've gleaned about God from church or family or culture. Additionally, in this approach the young people are afforded little control over the learning. Rather than processing the information in their own way, they're simply being asked to parrot back what they read in the Bible. In essence, they're reporting someone else's experience, rather than sharing an experience of their own.

In the second example, there's an intentional effort to tap into how the young people understand the character of God well before any direct instruction takes place. The *learning* part of the lesson happens because we start with what the teens already believe and help them connect the new learning to their established neural networks.

What Do I Think?

A multitude of techniques will help teenagers get in touch with what they think before you launch into the real content of a given lesson. Here are just a few examples:

Continuum: One nonthreatening way to get teens thinking about issues (without the fear of saying something stupid) is to indicate an imaginary line down the middle of the room. One end represents *agree,* the other is *disagree.* Make a statement related to your discussion topic and ask teens to place themselves somewhere along the invisible line to indicate how they feel about the statement.

Hypotheticals: Write up some very brief hypothetical situations that relate to your discussion and invite small groups to discuss their initial reactions and opinions.

Graffiti Wall: Put up large sheets of paper around the room, each with a different question written at the top. Invite youth to move from sheet to sheet writing or drawing their responses to the questions and looking at the responses of others.

Fishbowl: Sit in a circle and take turns pulling questions related to your topic out of a hat. Pass each question around the circle and invite individuals to respond with their own thoughts.

Vote: Have a mock election with a ballot that offers three or four ways of thinking about the issue you're discussing. Have everyone fill out the ballot at the beginning of the lesson, voting for the position they most agree with. You might even divide the group based on their votes and have them develop their arguments and give stump speeches.

Posters: Before discussing a particular issue, divide into small groups and have each one brainstorm how they might illustrate the topic graphically by creating a poster that promotes their ideas and questions.

Images: Display photographic images that relate to the issues you want teens to discuss. Ask them to select one (or more) that corresponds to their present feelings or thoughts and explain why they connected with those images.

Role-Play: If your teenagers are uncomfortable or shy about sharing their own thoughts, encourage them to role-play the thoughts of someone else.

First, create a persona for each participant. For example, you could write something like, "Cory is 18 years old and works for his dad. He has no plan to go to college when he graduates, so he doesn't see anything wrong with cheating on tests in order to pass his senior year." As you discuss the topic, invite group members to respond as their characters might.

Suggestion Box: Announce the topic for the discussion and ask your teens to think of any questions they might have about the issue. Invite them to write their questions on slips of paper and place them anonymously into a suggestion box. Then use these very questions as a way to guide the conversation.

These are just a few of the ideas we can use in youth ministry to help teens get in touch with their thinking and engage their brains as they answer that crucial question: *How does this new knowledge connect with my previous learning?*

Why Should I Care?

A second important question the teen brain asks when making connections is, *Why should I care about this?* Those who study the brain suggest that emotion drives attention. Think about your reactions when you watch a movie. Some movies simply fail to register with us emotionally, and we forget about them the moment we walk out of the theater. But other films—because they frighten us, thrill us, make us cry or laugh—stay with us for days or years to come. The hook here is our emotional reaction.

With that in mind, consider this fact: During adolescence the area of the brain that governs the emotions matures earlier than the area that governs reasoning. That means we ignore the emotional intelligence of young people at our own peril. In order for learning to take hold, we simply must help teens make emotional connections with their faith.

Believe it or not, for most teenagers Bible study isn't the most effective way to create emotional connections. A stroll through Revelation or an insightful look at the story of Bartimaeus isn't likely to cause a passionate response to bubble up out of your youth. But what if you started with something about which they're truly passionate?

Adolescence is a time when teens begin developing a heightened awareness of the world around them, particularly issues of injustice and need:

the global environmental crisis, poverty, child hunger, war, teen pregnancy, drug addiction, sex trafficking, the AIDS epidemic, and on and on. Starting your teaching time with issues that youth are passionate about—issues that evoke their feelings of concern, excitement, or even righteous indignation—can be an effective way to help them connect with biblical examples of Jesus' focus on justice, peace, and care for the outcast and neglected. By tapping into the emotions, we help the teen brain tune in to what we're saying and why they should care about this thing we call faith.

A word of caution here: As much as emotions drive attention, they can also cause the learning process to be derailed or manipulated. Challenge helps the brain to learn. But if a young person feels threatened, humiliated, or overly challenged, the portion of the brain that regulates fear (the amygdala) can hijack the brain by drawing attention away from learning in order to deal with the emotional need. You might see this in action if, in the middle of a Bible study, you suddenly pick on one of your teens and ask her to answer a really tough question. Caught off guard, and with every eye in the room upon her, she'll be afraid of looking foolish in front of her peers and literally withdraw and turn inward, becoming unwilling to speak. This is the amygdala kicking into action and turning attention away from learning in order to fight for emotional survival.

Many people, and not just introverts, are uncomfortable sharing their thoughts for fear of how others will react. One way to avoid this problem is to simply give your teens time to think through their responses. When posing a question to the group, invite teens to turn to a person next to them and take a minute or two to share their thoughts. Or allow time for them to write down their thoughts before sharing them. This gives each person some time to rehearse a response without the stress of blurting it out in front of the whole group.

When working with teens, we must create a learning environment that's emotionally and intellectually safe. Teenagers need to know they can share, doubt, question, and struggle without fear of ridicule or condemnation. Without a safe environment, learning connections are blocked and the journey of faith gets sidetracked.

Finally, be wary of manipulating teens' emotions in an effort to make a point, command their attention, or artificially force a spiritual decision. I've attended youth camps where the activities were clearly designed to progressively amp up the campers' emotions so that by the end of the week, all of the teenagers were crying and dreading a return to their normal lives. Some of those same youth who made tearful commitments to Christ on the last night of camp were the first ones to ditch church and youth group a week later in order to go to a friend's home to play video games. We want to appeal to the emotional intelligence of teens, but we want those emotions to be authentic and rise up out of a young person's genuine thoughts and experiences.

Teaching to Create Experiences

Oftentimes in youth ministry, we get the process of faith formation backward. We front-load our teaching with all sorts of information about Christian belief long before we offer our youth any real experience of faith. So many of our youth ministry gatherings are primarily focused on sitting around and talking, engaging issues of faith largely through Bible study or discussions.

> **Original Blog Date: April 27**
>
> I was recently reminded (like a two-by-four to the face) by one of my senior highers that youth group shouldn't focus on learning about Jesus so much as it should involve experiencing firsthand the way Jesus loved and lived. Bible studies and discussions are fine, but our real focus should be on helping youth experience what it means to love and be loved, to serve and be served in the way Jesus has set before us. —Brian

Think of Jesus' own ministry as portrayed in Scripture. Consider his encounters with the woman at the well, the tax collector Zacchaeus, the children who sat on his knee, the 10 lepers, the paralyzed man lowered through a hole in the roof . Over and over again, those who met Jesus encountered an experience of his compassion, his healing, his peace, his love, and his radical way of seeing the world long before they encountered his teachings. Jesus didn't insist that Bartimaeus listen to a sermon before being healed. He didn't ask the 5,000 to engage in a Bible study before he fed them with a couple of fish and loaves of bread. Repeatedly we see in Scripture that it's an experience that opens hearts and allows individuals to be vulnerable enough to learn more about God and faith.

Think back to your childhood for a minute. When you remember your time in youth ministry as a teen—or perhaps camp or Sunday school or worship—what comes to mind first? The lessons you were taught? The sermons you heard? The Bible studies you endured? No. More likely, such a memory trip causes your brain to conjure up images of experiences: the mission trip to the inner city, prayers around the campfire, singing in the youth choir, community-building games, the Youth Sunday when you served at the Communion table. These experiences helped your brain make the abstract teachings of faith real.

Given this realization, wouldn't we be better off putting our time and energy into developing more hands-on ministry opportunities for youth—experiences that get them off the couches of our youth rooms and out into the mission field? Then they might actually have something to sit down and talk about.

Rather than talking about homelessness, your group could partner with a local shelter to actually meet and develop a relationship with people who live on the street every day. Instead of talking about hunger, your group could experience a 24-hour fast to understand what it's like to go without food. Instead of talking about poverty, you could take a mission trip to the inner city and serve clients in a soup kitchen or work with children in a low-income daycare program. Instead of just talking about Jesus' healing ministry, you could take a road trip to a nursing home or a hospital and visit with residents and patients. Rather than just talking about hospitality and welcoming the stranger, your group could go out into the community and spend an afternoon raking lawns or hauling trash or helping an older person work in her garden.

Learning Styles

We can create meaningful experiences right in our own youth rooms and church sanctuaries as well. However, we must be sensitive to the different ways our teenagers interact with the world around them. Perhaps it goes without saying, but not all people learn in the same way. Though sitting on the floor in a circle and talking about issues may really engage some young people, for others it will be a complete bore. Creating learning experiences that will activate the teenage brain demands that we be attentive to the different learning styles in our groups.

There are three primary learning styles:

- Visual—those who learn best through their eyes
- Auditory—those who learn best through their ears
- Tactile or Kinesthetic—those who learn best through touch and manipulation of their environment

We do fairly well attending to the auditory learners in our churches. (Think about how much listening we're asked to do in a typical worship service.) But we often neglect the visual and kinesthetic learners.

Yet at the same time, I know some youth workers who are particularly good at providing active learning time for teens. These leaders know that young people want to be part of the action and interact with the lesson. Jacob provides great interactive talks in his youth group worship times. And for years my brother Barry has offered keynote talks at church camps that are much more than just *talks*. He crams them full of illustrations, questions, Q&A, visual props, simulations, dramas, and audience participation—and the teenagers eat it up. These leaders understand the challenge to engage all three learning styles as much as possible.

I wonder if it would surprise you to know how often the Bible shows Jesus taking this very approach.

Original Blog Date: February 3

As with most Saturdays that come before a preaching Sunday, I find myself wondering if there isn't a better way. What is this thing we do called "preaching"? Who came up with this idea of a pastor standing in front of the congregation for 15 to 20 minutes (or more), reading from a prepared text, offering up one person's reading and (possibly) Spirit-inspired interpretation of Scripture? I know the notion of the three-point speech (so beloved of clergy) goes back to Plato, so it's hardly a biblical approach to passing on the faith.

So I'm intrigued by this week's Gospel lesson (Luke 5:1-11) that depicts Jesus teaching the people while he sits on a boat out on the water (not pontificating from a pulpit-on-high). At one point he incorporates an object lesson of sorts by challenging Simon Peter and the other fishermen to put out on the lake and go fishing. In my educator days, this is what we called "active learning": involving your teenager, body and soul, in the act of meaning making. Would the lesson about the abundance of the kingdom have hit home so hard if Jesus had simply talked about it, rather than letting them experience it for themselves? —Brian

Have you ever noticed how Jesus attends to the various learning styles in this passage? For the auditory learners, his amazing public-speaking skills serve to capture their interest. For the visual learners, he creates the unusual sight of their teacher speaking to them from a small boat on the water. For the kinesthetic learners, he issues the challenge for them to come out onto the water themselves and cast their nets as a way to experience the abundance of God's kingdom firsthand. Jesus engaged people through all of their senses and through the many ways his followers experienced the world. What might happen if we took the same approach to teaching our young people?

Many years ago I wanted to get my youth ministry to really dig into the problem of homelessness. The teens in my group all came from middle- or upper-middle-class families and grew up in a small town where the homeless are mostly invisible. To make the issue more real for them, our youth ministry team decided to challenge the youth to spend the night in our church parking lot. And the teens were allowed to bring only a sleeping bag and a pillow.

With a complete attitude of seriousness about this experiment, the teenagers spent the first part of the evening digging through dirty, smelly dumpsters to find cardboard and plastic for building a shanty in which to sleep. Later in the evening, a church member drove up and served us cold sandwiches and water out of the back of her car. We even arranged for the police to come by late at night to shine lights into our makeshift homes as we tried to sleep. The experiment ended early Sunday morning when it suddenly started pouring rain, and those of us with poorly constructed shanties found ourselves soaking wet. So we raced into the church to seek shelter in the comfort of our youth room.

Afterward, as we discussed the experience, I could tell it wasn't lost on the group that truly homeless people don't have a cozy, warm church to run to when it starts to rain. For the visual learners, the sights of that night (cardboard shelters, dinner from a car trunk, police cars, and morning rainstorms) ensured that their brains were hooked by the experience. For the auditory learners, the conversations that took place as we struggled to build our shantytown, the sounds of traffic going by as we slept in the parking lot, and the thunder and pouring rain etched the experience into conscious thought. For the tactile or kinesthetic learners, using their hands to dig through a dumpster and build a shanty, sleeping on hard asphalt, and racing to the church to escape the storm helped them experience the issue of homelessness in a way that a chat in the youth room never could.

Even today, those teenagers tell me they remember that night—the way it gave them a taste of the vulnerability of life on the street, and the sense of empathy they developed for *the least of these*. By attending to the various learning styles of our young people, we helped them learn more about the call of faith on their lives.

Of course not every learning experience can be quite as involved as a night spent sleeping on asphalt. But we can attend to the various learning styles in many other ways—both great and small:

- Provide art supplies to help teenagers explore a topic or issue.
- Play songs that connect with the discussion topic.
- Incorporate pantomime, role-playing, and drama.
- Engage in debates on a topic.
- Invite the teens to close their eyes and imagine a Bible story as you read it aloud.

However we choose to attend to the various learning styles, our goal should always be to help young people extend their learning beyond the pages of Scripture, beyond the comfort of the youth room, and into the multitude of ways they experience life.

Teaching to Encourage Reflection

Helping teens explore the ways their faith connects with the rest of their lives and their emotional experience of the world is a large part of our calling as youth leaders. But if all we offer are experiences, then we've fought only half the battle. For these experiences to really take hold and change the hearts of teens, we have to help them engage in a process of thoughtful reflection and meaning making. Sometimes this process happens on its own, but more often young people will need our guidance to make sense of the thoughts and emotions that are swirling around inside their heads.

The most effective way to encourage reflection is by simply offering teens more time:

- Teens need time to rest their brains after an engaging lesson. Twenty minutes of instruction is about the limit before the brain needs a break.
- Teens need time to think about new information before deciding what to do with it. Expecting an immediate response or commitment can derail the reflection process.
- Teens need time to try new ideas. Encouraging teens to live out what they've learned during the coming week aids in the process of meaning making.
- Teens need time to ask and answer questions.

This last item may be the most effective way to challenge the brain to work at meaning making. And asking questions seemed to be one of Jesus' favorite teaching methods. Scripture is full of stories about Jesus posing questions as a way to get his listeners to imagine a new reality.

In Mark 8:29, Jesus challenges his disciples by asking, "Who do you say I am?" Following his story of the good Samaritan, Jesus doesn't end with a sermon but a question: "Which of these three, do you think, was a neighbour to the man who fell into the hands of the robbers?" (Luke 10:36

NRSV). When Jesus heals the paralyzed man and notices that the scribes are critical of his actions, he responds, "Which is easier, to say to the paralytic, 'Your sins are forgiven', or to say, 'Stand up and take your mat and walk'?" (Mark 2:9 NRSV). He leaves those questions hanging in the air for both the scribes and the other people to ponder.

Beyond Yes or No Responses

Asking questions that invite reflection takes some effort. If you think back to your own school days, you might recall that most of the questions were factual—or what educators call *closed*. Closed questions either have one right answer or require a yes or no response. These sorts of questions have their place. But if we truly want youth to think for themselves and engage in honest reflection about their faith, then we need to make use of more open-ended questions:

Divergent questions: These questions push teenagers to consider what might have happened. They have to move away from the text or the conversation and think about the bigger picture: *How do you think Martha felt after Jesus told her to let Mary sit at his knee? What sorts of people did Jesus encounter whom others considered outcasts? What are your favorite places to pray?*

Comparative questions: These questions encourage young people to draw on information from a variety of resources or experiences: *How do you see Jesus' view of religion to be different from that of the Pharisees? In what ways were the practices of the early church similar or different from Jesus' teachings? How is our youth ministry like or unlike the other clubs and groups to which you belong?*

Speculative questions: These questions invite some imagination about the present or future: *What do you think happened to the injured man after the Samaritan left him at the inn? What do you imagine would happen if the government outlawed religion? If Jesus were here, what do you believe he'd say about the church today?*

Evaluative questions: These questions encourage the learner to make a personal value judgment: *What do you think about the problem of teen alcohol abuse? What's the most important part of being a Christian? How would you decide whether or not our country should fight a war?*

The most important thing about all of these types of questions is that there is no one right answer. Each one invites teenagers to ponder, dream, wonder, speculate, and imagine. Each challenges the participant to work at making connections, consider what's most important in his or her life, and actively engage in the learning process. Each has the potential to invite young people to start digging in the field of faith for their own treasure, while encouraging us to be their companions as they search for meaning.

Join Teens in the Journey

The more I rethink the traditional approaches to teaching and learning in youth ministry, the more I'm convinced that the way forward must involve youth leaders seeing themselves in missional ministry *with* youth—as a minister among ministers, serving alongside teens and joining them in their journey of faith.

As followers of the way of Christ, we're challenged to let the children come among us, to learn from them, to accept the gifts of ministry they have to offer us, and to see them as fellow travelers on the journey of faith. To accept such a challenge, I suspect, would require many churches to scrap their present youth programming, to reexamine their methods of Christian education, and to reconsider what it means to help youth seek their own faithful response to the way of Christ. In doing so, we just might find ourselves creating new and exciting opportunities in the church where youth can make their journey toward an authentic faith that makes the transforming love of God in Christ real.

Jacob's Reflections

Several years ago my wife and I led groups of middle schoolers on backpacking trips in Colorado. We'd spend an entire week hiking in the mountains, filtering our own water, hanging our food bags in trees to avoid bears, and praying to God while the beauty of the mountains towered over us. For those seven days, our group was a very intense community of Christ.

I remember the uncertainty and anxiety of those trips. As soon as we arrived at the trailhead, everyone—including the adults—had lots of questions: *What will the trip be like? Will I be able to make it? Will I grow spiritually? Will I get along with the others?* But as soon as those first few miles were behind us and the blisters were tended to, the fears and anxiety began to dissipate. When you're on your own in the middle of the wilderness, you quickly learn the importance of working together.

In a sense the process of teaching and learning in youth ministry isn't much different than a backpacking trip. As you journey together, the same questions we had at the trailhead will arise. But instead of feeding the anxiety, try taking a renewed approach to the spiritual journey with your young people.

As we trekked through the mountains of Colorado, we had definite beginning and ending points. The distance between Point A and Point B was roughly 10 miles. A number of the group members had maps, compasses, even a GPS. But as we walked those miles, it became clear that we weren't going along a straight path. We zig-zagged back and forth all over the mountains. There were plenty of tears, frustrations, and, by the end, huge rewards. The same is true with youth ministry.

Instead of seeing your journey with youth as a particular destination with a clearly defined path, spend some time rethinking how you walk the journey. Take the time to navigate like the ancient sailors did—using the stars as a guiding point. Use your unique gifts as a rudder for your ministry, while anticipating the inevitable series of turns and unpredictable difficulties.

Rethinking Your Own Ministry

- Reflect on your teaching style. What's your dominant approach to sharing information with your teens?

- Which learning styles have you observed in the teens you serve? Which learning styles are neglected in your teaching approach? How might you adapt your teaching to tap into these different styles?

- How much room is there in your ministry for teens to ask questions? How might you encourage teens to ask more questions?

- Reflect back on your recent studies and discussions. What role, if any, did the group members play in determining the topics and content to be studied? In what ways could you involve them more in the process?

- Brainstorm ideas for turning your next Bible study into a Bible experience. How could you help your teens explore the story or theme with all of their senses?

chapter 8

worship that connects

Brian

Growing up as a preacher's kid, my childhood and youth were steeped in hymn singing, stained-glass windows, choir robes, liturgical prayers, and all the other trappings of mainline church worship. By the fourth grade, I could sing "The Old Rugged Cross" by heart, I knew every word of the Apostle's Creed, and church was like a second home to me. Unlike many kids my age, I enjoyed being there and understood it to be an important part of my family's life.

Yet when we headed home on Sunday afternoons, in my mind we left God behind. It never occurred to me to consider that God might be present outside of formal worship. I never thought about the possibility of making worship part of my daily routine, my interactions with friends at school, or my time at home with my family.

Original Blog Date: November 10

In the exile the Israelites came to understand that God didn't dwell in just one particular place but that God's presence could be experienced anywhere. Yet how many of our teens believe that worshipping God mostly happens in the confines of a church sanctuary one hour a week? —Brian

By high school my perspective began to shift. Through the mentorship of some excellent Sunday school teachers, I began to develop a relationship with a God who wasn't confined to the four walls of the sanctuary. I began to understand my connection with the God who speaks to the prophet Jeremiah: "Am I a God near by, says the LORD, and not a God far off? Who can hide in secret places so that I cannot see them? says the LORD. Do I not fill heaven and earth? says the LORD" (Jeremiah 23:23-24 NRSV). I believe it's *that* God—a God who's present with us in all of life—who young people want to worship with passion and devotion.

Keeping It Real

Teenagers want to know and worship a God who spends time with them beyond the confines of stained glass and organ music. They want a God who meets them in the messiness of their daily lives. They want to worship a God who is real. That means we need to offer them worship experiences that are real.

We can do that by keeping that word—*real*—in mind. Think of real worship as being **R**elational, **E**xperiential, **A**we-filled, and **L**ife-changing—REAL. Here's what that might look like.

Relational. At its very core, Christianity is a communal faith. When worship becomes a solitary act that's just about our personal relationship with God, we miss the experience of finding God in our relationships with one another. In Matthew's Gospel Jesus challenges any private and individualistic notion of worship when he declares, "'You shall love the Lord your God with all your heart, and with all your soul, and with all your mind.' This is the greatest and first commandment. And a second is like it: 'You shall love your neighbour as yourself'" (Matthew 22:37-39 NRSV). I truly believe young people are seeking intimacy in worship. They want to connect on a personal level—with God, with each other, and with the created world. Helping youth find God in fellowship and in community can give them new eyes to seek God in all of their relationships.

Experiential: Everything that takes place in worship is considered liturgy. In Greek the word for *liturgy* means "work of the people." But so much of what we consider to be worship is passive with participants acting like audience members at a play. How much worship time is spent simply sitting and watching others lead music, preach a sermon, offer a prayer? Yet the Bible gives witness to story after story of people experiencing God's presence in active ways—pillars of cloud and fire, visitations of heavenly messengers, the healing and compassion of Jesus, the tongues and flames of Pentecost.

The biblical God is not an abstract idea but a tangible presence revealed in shared meals, conversations on hillsides, and walks down dusty roads. The apostle Paul encourages us to "pray without ceasing" (1 Thessalonians 5:17 NRSV). Certainly he doesn't mean we're to spend our lives sitting in pews with our heads bowed and hands folded. To pray without ceasing—to worship without ceasing—is a call to connect with God with our whole beings and in all of the activities of our lives. This is the spirit of worship we need to cultivate in our teenagers.

Awe-filled: The writer of Psalm 8 looks into the night sky and is overwhelmed by the awesomeness of God's presence in creation. The psalmist writes of a God who is larger than our imaginations, yet desires to know us intimately. Teens want to connect with a God who helps them see the world through eyes of wonder. We can lead youth in experiences of awe by encouraging them to seek the sacred everywhere—not just in the sanctuary, but also in the nighttime sky, in a quiet moment with a friend, in the act of creating art. We can lead young people to experience awe by helping them see the youth group—everything from the youth room to their church friends—as sacred because it helps them encounter God's love, peace, hope, and grace.

Life-changing: Not all worship experiences can be like the sky opening up and a dove coming down from the heavens. But worship does have the potential to help us see the world through God's eyes and imagine it as it could be. Think of the way Zacchaeus (Luke 19:1-10) is changed over a meal with Jesus, or the way Lydia is changed during a conversation with the disciples (Acts 16:14-15). Worship provides a window for youth to see the inbreaking of God's kingdom all around them. It invites them to be part of God's transformation of the world.

When we offer teens worship experiences that are relational, experiential, awe-filled, and life-changing, we're helping them see God as an ever-present part of their lives. It's in these moments that teenagers just might be *caught* by God.

Getting Caught

Original Blog Date: April 12

Several weeks ago, during Lent, I preached on a text that describes Peter's call to ministry. It's that well-known passage where Jesus tells Peter and the other guys to drop their nets out in the deep water, even though they'd fished all night and come up empty-handed. Peter has his doubts but does it anyway. Of course they bring in a huge catch of fish, and Peter prostrates himself before Jesus, declaring himself a sinner. Jesus tells him to get up, to stop being so afraid, and to help him catch other people.

In the sermon I suggested that in that moment of grace and understanding from Jesus (and in that moment of experiencing the abundance of the kingdom, as symbolized by the catch of fish), Peter is caught by Christ. I then challenged the congregation to consider when in their lives they'd been caught, realizing that this isn't a singular event, but rather an existential experience, happening moment-to-moment as we open ourselves up to recognizing and embodying the love and grace of God through Christ. I even invited the congregation to write their experiences of being caught on small paper fish, which they then brought forward and placed on the Communion table. —Brian

The responses we received to that worship experience point to the great diversity of ways in which we each experience God's presence. Worshippers wrote about being caught by God at church camp, or through a relationship with a loved one, in a moment of silence, during worship, in the act of Communion, and even during a walk in the woods. Those who felt they hadn't yet been caught were invited to write a prayer asking God to open them up to the possibility.

A week or so after that worship service, I was spending time with some of the younger teenagers in our church as they prepared for their upcoming baptisms. One young man shared that he finally made the decision to be baptized during my *fishy* sermon about being caught by Christ. He decided that he'd indeed been caught and it was time to respond to that experience.

The testimony of this young person reminded me of the importance of creating room for meaningful worship in the lives of our young people. It's not about converting them or indoctrinating them with our theology or adding to the number of people filling our pews on Sunday mornings. Worship can and should be about providing spaces and places and times in the lives of teens in which they can experience God's love and grace so palpably that they too can say, "I've been caught. Now show me how to help others get caught, too."

The challenge that so many youth workers face is that our congregations often expect youth to get caught by God while sitting through Sunday morning or midweek worship services. Certainly young people have many options for finding a worship style that fits their needs. Some churches offer high liturgical worship, some offer low-church praise services, and some even create energetic, techno-savvy worship experiences that resemble rock concerts. But ultimately these worship experiences are predominantly passive experiences—we sit and receive worship like an audience member watching a Broadway musical.

This approach to worship is fine if you primarily process the world through your ears or eyes. But as I mentioned in chapter 7, teenagers explore their world and learn in a variety of ways. If we want to offer them meaningful opportunities for worship, we're going to have to rethink our ideas about what worship can be.

What Worship Can Be

It's helpful for youth workers to be aware that not everyone learns in the same way. In the previous chapter, I touched on the three primary learning styles: visual, auditory, and tactile or kinesthetic. While they have clear application to the educational piece of our ministries, they have just as much relevance to the way we think about worship.

The growing body of literature around the theory of multiple intelligences reminds us that different brains respond to different learning environments and experiences. Some of us are drawn to the use of our hands, some use our voices, some use our ears. Some love silence and some would rather be outdoors. There are those of us who learn best in groups, and others learn better when they're alone. This same understanding of learning could be applied to our individual experience of worship and prayer as we seek to connect with God. When it comes to the efficacy of worship and prayer, one size does not fit all.

The worship and prayer ideas that follow are each tied to one or more of the multiple intelligences. These ideas could be adapted to use as stand-alone prayer centers or as part of a worship service. Many will work just as well outdoors as indoors. I've used them in settings from summer camp to retreat weekends to regular weekly youth group gatherings. Each idea is fairly open-ended and can be adapted to a particular theme or scriptural focus. Most importantly they're designed to help teenagers connect with God.

After each activity invite your group members to share their reactions to the experience. There is no right or wrong answer to the outcome of these activities, so the best way to follow up is to ask, "What did you feel? What did you think about? What did you learn?" Just keep in mind that the point of these activities can simply be the experience itself and the time youth spend in prayer and contemplation. You don't have to have a big discussion every time.

1. Bodily-Kinesthetic Intelligence

This intelligence involves a tendency to experience the world through touch and movement. Worship that connects with this kind of intelligence includes—

- Walking: If you've ever walked a labyrinth, you know it can offer a particularly rich spiritual experience. As you walk the path, you pass others or they pass you. You walk at your own pace and others walk at theirs. You seem to be working your way toward the center and suddenly find yourself on the outside of the design. Finally you reach the center, pause, and start your journey back to the beginning. Even though you're retracing your steps, going in the other direction makes the path completely new. All of this whispers metaphorically of the spiritual journey we walk together. Give your teenagers a chance to walk a labyrinth—you can create your own or find one in your area—so they can use their bodies as they pray and reflect on their faith.

- Sculpting: In Genesis 1 God gives human beings the charge to be the stewards or caretakers of creation. In Genesis 2 God gives the first human complete creative responsibility for naming all the animals. In the process of naming, a human being helps form the identities of the earth's creatures. These stories speak of the way we're invited to join with God in the continuing story of growing, building, developing, and caring for creation. Creating art can be a reminder of this Genesis call to partner with God in the ongoing creation of the world. Consider providing a variety of materials such as craft dough, pipe cleaners, or tinfoil. Invite your teenagers to create a mini-sculpture to represent a particular prayer need, joy, or concern. As they finish they can add their creations to others', then contemplate and lift up all the other prayers that have been depicted.

- Eating: Taste is a sense that we rarely tap into as part of worship. Look for ways to tie food into the experience, such as using fresh-baked bread and grapes for Communion, or offering teens the chance to taste foods that would have been common in Jesus' lifetime. You could even replace the traditional Communion elements and instead share in a real meal together as you recall and celebrate the meaning of Communion.

2. Verbal-Linguistic Intelligence

This intelligence involves a comfort with expressing oneself through language, either written or spoken. Ideas for connecting worship with this intelligence include—

- Letters: Set out several game boards and an assortment of letter blocks from games like Scrabble®. Ask your group to reflect on how they know and experience God. Invite them to offer a prayer of thanks for God's presence in their lives, by using the letters to create words on the game board that describe God. They may want to connect their words—

Scrabble®-style—to other teens' words, symbolizing the way in which our different experiences of God come together in community.

- Chalkboard: Provide each person with a small chalkboard, chalk, and an eraser. Have them spend time writing down the things in their lives for which they're seeking forgiveness. This could be just a list of items, or it could be in the form of a letter or poem. After praying for openness to God's forgiveness, have teens erase what they've written on the chalkboard as a symbol of reconciliation with God.

- Scripture: It might seem obvious to use Scripture as part of a worship experience, but there are creative ways to encourage teenagers to explore a text more deeply. *Lectio Divina*, or *sacred reading*, is an ancient Christian practice of reading a biblical text in a way that allows it to speak to us more intimately. Suggest a text and encourage each person to read the passage three times slowly, in silence. The first time they should read the passage for its overall content. The second time they should try to tune in to a word or phrase that seems to speak directly to them in some way. The third time they should try to discern what God might be saying to them through the text. Ask those who feel comfortable doing so to talk about what stood out to them. This process isn't rushed—silence and reflection is as important as the reading of the text.

- Rewrite: Sometimes the best way to connect with God's Word is to try to express the text in our own words. Invite teens to take a common passage, such as the Lord's Prayer (Luke 11), and rewrite it in their own words.

3. Logical-Mathematical Intelligence

This intelligence relates to our ability to learn through logic, patterns, sequences, and numbers. Ideas for connecting worship with this intelligence include—

- Puzzle: Set up a prayer station that includes a cross-shaped tangram puzzle—you can find templates for these on the Internet. Ask teens to take their time piecing together the puzzle and meditating on what the challenge of the cross means to them.

- Compare and Contrast: Helping youth to engage with the Bible through critical analysis can lead to a deeper connection with the power of the gospel. Invite teens to explore the same story in two or more of the Gospels, such as the two narratives surrounding Jesus' birth in Matthew and Luke. Challenge them to look for both the similarities and differences and to consider why the writers tell the story in their particular way.

4. Visual-Spatial Intelligence

This intelligence is often demonstrated through the creation or appreciation of visual images and art. Ideas for connecting worship with this intelligence include—

- Draw-a-Prayer: We're so accustomed to praying with words alone that the opportunity to express prayer through art can be a freeing experience for young people. Provide paper and various drawing supplies and invite your teens to create expressions of prayers using only images and symbols. You might encourage your group to focus on a particular topic, such as the world or peace or hurt.
- Images: Put together a digital slide presentation of images related to your worship or study theme and then set the images to loop. Provide comfortable chairs so people can simply sit and meditate on the pictures. This approach can be particularly effective when the images are black-and-white photos or classical or sacred artworks.
- Group Art: A group art experience can draw a worshipping community together in a powerful way as each person adds to the contributions of others. I once led a worship experience in which we invited the group to create a mural highlighting some of the foundational elements of youth ministry: friends, family, fellowship, and faith. With no prior planning, the teens began painting the mural on a large canvas spread on the floor. They painted symbols, words, abstract images, swaths of color—whatever came to mind that might help illustrate the theme of the night. They were encouraged to add on to, or even paint on top of, each other's efforts as the mural took shape organically. To add one more little wrinkle, we explained that to illustrate the way we

each bring unique and special gifts to our ministry, each person was given something different to paint with. Some had brushes; others had ladles, sponges, or toothbrushes. We even had a few teens use their hands or feet.

5. Musical-Rhythmic Intelligence

This intelligence is often demonstrated through the appreciation of sound or the performance of music. Ideas for connecting worship with this intelligence include—

- Lyrics: The Psalms witness to the importance of song in worship. Lyrics set to music have the power to evoke a worshipful attitude in a way the spoken word can't. Make several playlists on an MP3 player with hymns, contemporary Christian songs, or Gregorian chants. Invite your group to spend some time focusing on the emotions and messages of the music.
- Melody: Different styles of music can change the focus of our worship. Try playing a series of wordless melodies from different musical styles, such as classical, jazz, hip-hop, or reggae. Challenge your group to focus on reading a particular Scripture text as they listen. Ask them to note how the different musical styles affect their thoughts and insights about the passage.
- Confession: The sound for this worship experience is the noise of a grinding paper shredder. Set up an area with paper, pens, and the shredder. Have everyone write about the broken places in their lives, attitudes, and habits they want to change, or relationships that need healing. Then have them run their written confessions through the shredder. As they do, invite them to offer a prayer asking God for forgiveness and release from all that has them in bondage.

6. Interpersonal Intelligence

This intelligence is expressed in an ability to work with and relate to other people and groups. Ideas for connecting worship with this intelligence include—

- Mandala: This prayer practice invites a small group to work together to create a *sacred circle*. Give each group a large piece of paper and have them draw either one large circle or a set of concentric circles. Then have each person draw, paint, or write prayer concerns and joys inside the circle. If you like, guide the experience by inviting teens to reflect first on their daily lives, then on their spiritual lives, and finally on how they hear God's calling. The advantage of this approach is that groups create together, each adding or responding to the contributions of others.

- Acrostic: Encourage youth to work together to create an acrostic poem related to the worship or prayer theme. Choose a single word such as *forgiveness* and write it in large letters down the left side of a sheet of paper. Have teens take turns writing one line of the poem at a time, with the first word in each line starting with one letter of the word.

7. Intrapersonal Intelligence

This intelligence involves private introspection. Ideas for connecting worship with this intelligence include—

- Photos: Provide teens with a collection of photos or images of sacred art. Ask them to spend some time in private thought, focusing on the images that speak to them or that help them lift up particular prayers of need, thanks, or praise. Use the images to focus your group's thoughts with questions such as, "Which image most connects with your understanding of God's grace?"

- *Ignatian Examen*: In its simplest form, this Christian prayer practice invites individuals to let their minds wander to those places where they've seen and felt God's presence in their lives. Ask your young people to think back over the recent past, focusing on moments when they were grateful and moments when they felt dissatisfied. Ask, "At what moments did you give and receive God's love the most?" or "When did you give and receive love the least?" or "When were you paying the most attention to the love of God in the world? When were you paying the least attention?" Finish by thanking God for the gift of today and ask for guidance in being more open to God's presence in your daily lives.

- Silence: For most of us, silence is a rare experience. The same can be said for worship, as every second is often filled with music and words. But if prayer is a conversation, then we also need silence so we can listen. Jesus knew the value of going off to a quiet place to pray. For some teenagers this practice might be the most effective way for them to focus on God's presence. Provide space for teens to be alone and pillows for those who want to sit on the floor or lie down. Allow for a long period of unbroken silence in which they can simply listen for God's voice. If total silence is too much, provide background sounds of flowing water or gentle rain.

8. Naturalist Intelligence

This intelligence involves a sensitivity to nature. Ideas for connecting worship with this intelligence include—

- Nature Walk: Invite group members to take a stroll outside, noting the gifts of creation all around them and offering a prayer of thanks for each. As they walk they should look for a natural object—a leaf, a rock, a flower—that symbolizes God for them. Ask each person to bring their object back to the prayer room if they can. Create an altar where teens can place their objects as reminders of God's presence in creation.

- Water: Water is a prominent symbol throughout the Bible. The sound of pouring water, the taste of cold water, the sensation of water on our skin can draw us into biblical stories of cleansing and renewal, as well as conjure up memories of baptism. Set up a space with a large bowl and pitcher of water. Have each person offer a silent prayer as they pour a small amount of water into the bowl, either directly from the pitcher or through the hands of another person. Invite the group to consider how their prayers have mixed together in the water as a symbol of the life they share with one another as brothers and sisters in Christ.

- Stones: Assemble a collection of smooth stones and permanent markers. Ask participants to choose a stone and hold it firmly in their hands, focusing on and praying for a particular joy or concern. After a time of prayer, have them write a word or phrase on the stone to represent their prayers. Then create a cairn—a stack of stones that serves as a reminder of God's care and faithfulness.

• Branches: Provide a pile of sticks and branches and invite the group to work together to form a sculpture with them. You could have each stick represent an individual prayer, while the sculpture represents how our prayers are connected to each other. Or you could have the entire sculpture represent a prayer. This idea works as well indoors as outdoors. In some ways it's even more striking indoors as the natural sculpture contrasts with the artificiality of an inside space.

Of course, any of these prayer experiences can be enhanced by reading Scripture, playing sacred music in the background, or creating written questions to encourage thought and meditation in a prayer journal. As I mentioned earlier, you may want to debrief with your group after using these creative approaches to worship, or you may want the experiences to speak for themselves. If you choose the latter, you can still learn a great deal about how your teens were impacted by the experience by looking at the images, written reflections, art, and other artifacts they leave behind at the prayer centers.

Connecting to the Whole Church

I began this discussion of worship by suggesting that we need to help young people develop an understanding of worship that goes beyond the boundaries of the sanctuary walls. However, I don't want to leave you with the impression that we should do away with youth participation in organized congregational worship. The symbols, liturgies, and spiritual practices that have been part of the Christian church since ancient times still hold incredible potential to help youth connect with and find their center in the heart of God. Involving youth in the regular worship experiences of the church can be an important part of helping teenagers find their place within the wider body of Christ.

That said, I couldn't end this chapter without saying just a little about that unique Christian tradition that in many churches counts as the one time of the year when youth are integrated into adult worship: Youth Sunday.

Original Blog Date: September 21

I recently communicated with a blogger friend . . . about how to organize a Youth Sunday. Our conversation got me thinking about why I just don't like Youth Sundays. And I can sum it up in one word: *Gimmick.*

Years ago, before most of you were born, this country was forced to endure the release of a gangster movie called *Bugsy Malone.* But this was no ordinary gangster movie. It had a huge gimmick: All the parts were played by kids! And instead of the guns shooting bullets, they shot cream pies. How many of us have "Bugsy Maloned" the annual Youth Sunday service by replacing all of the adults with teenagers? And how many of us have helmed Youth Sundays where the Communion elements were replaced with something like soda pop and goldfish crackers? That's the Bugsy-Malone-cream-pie-gun version of Communion. Do you see the problem here? This let-the-youth-take-over-for-one-Sunday-and-do-whatever-they-want approach is too susceptible to being seen as a gimmick. And something that's seen as a gimmick is often not taken seriously. —Brian

So what would I suggest instead? When planning a Youth Sunday service, encourage teenagers to respect the basic format of your established worship service while infusing it with their own particular gifts. This may mean they sing or perform the music, write the prayers, or deliver the sermon. Make the planning of the service intergenerational. Arrange for the members of your group to work with your regular worship team or the pastor—and ask your pastor to consider having a few teenagers help create the morning's sermon, possibly even as a dialogue with the pastor. Encourage them to involve other adults in the service as liturgists, musicians, ushers, and so on.

Challenge your teens to remember that worship should be designed to be meaningful to all ages and allow all who are present to worship God without being tripped up by the form of the service. (Translation: If using gummy worms in place of the Communion bread will keep someone from coming to the table, it might be worth a second thought.)

This sort of approach could set the tone for a Youth Sunday that's less gimmicky and more of a celebration of intergenerational leadership in the church. In fact it just might set a new standard for how worship is designed and led from that day forward. Perhaps there will no longer be a need for Youth Sundays because youth will be involved intentionally, creatively, and meaningfully in worship and connection with God all year long!

My early days as a preacher's kid started me off on the right track for a life of connectedness with and a commitment to God as shown to us in the life of Christ. But had I never moved beyond that childlike way of believing that worship and God belonged only in the church, I don't know if I'd still be an active Christian today.

The church has to answer the call of young people who want a relationship with the sacred that goes beyond pews and hymnals and altar calls. When we help teens experience that sacredness in all of life, we help them develop a practice of prayer and worship that can be deeply relational, deeply rooted in the experiences of life, full of awe and wonder, and completely life-changing.

Jacob's Reflections

It was the second day of camp. At breakfast we shared with the campers how each afternoon there would be a variety of focus groups to choose from: hiking, swimming, sporting activities, crafts, and Scripture study. And there was also going to be a new activity that year—guided prayer and meditation. We expected the swimming to fill up first, followed quickly by the sporting events.

So you can imagine how surprised the camp counselors were when guided prayer and meditation was the first focus group to fill up completely. In fact each day we had a line of sixth and seventh grade teens asking to experience the guided meditation even though the class was already full. Of course we found a way to include everyone.

The session for the prayer and meditation was simple. We started with some calming music—I think we played something from Enya. Next we asked the participants to get comfortable and focus on their breathing, encouraging them to breathe deeply, in and out. Then we asked them to envision a place where they felt completely welcome and at peace. Using guided imagery, we asked them to remember as many details as they could. We asked: "What do you see? What do you smell? What do you hear? Are you moving? Are you sitting? Is anyone else with you? What does the sky look like? What does the sun feel like?" The entire meditation took close to 45 minutes. And, throughout the entire week's meditation sessions, I never once had to ask a teenager to be quiet or stop goofing off.

Following each session, we spent a few minutes sharing and debriefing on what we'd experienced. Immediately I was struck by how many of these middle schoolers said these sessions were their favorite part of the day. When asked why they enjoyed the prayer and meditation so much, many of them said that because of the busyness of their lives, there was very little time to slow down and connect with God. Together we spent some time brainstorming how they could continue to practice these prayer exercises at home.

That week of camp solidified for me the belief that young people are yearning for a deeper experience with God. They look to their leaders for new ways to experience the depth and breadth of God's transforming love and grace. As we plan worship experiences for youth, we can't be afraid to embrace the silence. We can't be afraid to ask youth to experience God in new ways while remembering to be still and listen to the voice of God.

Rethinking Your Own Ministry

- Spend some time as a youth ministry team defining the word *worship*. Consider how, where, and why it happens in your setting.

- Which of the multiple intelligences are most often engaged in your worship experiences? How might you offer more worship opportunities for teens to use their bodies, incorporate art, engage different musical styles, use critical thinking, or connect with nature?

- Consider new ways to allow teens to experience silence and contemplation as a form of worship.

- When designing a Youth Sunday, how might you make it an intergenerational experience for the teenagers?

- Explore some of the contemplative ancient Christian spiritual practices with your teenagers. Consider adopting one or more of them as a regular part of your worship time together.

chapter 9

creating a missional ministry

Really? Did you really believe that after all our talk about creating a missional model of youth ministry, we'd just hand you a cookie-cutter program?

The truth is we were tempted. We were tempted to lay out exactly how we structure a typical Sunday evening youth group. We were tempted to explain our approach to leading youth events—from the opening game to the closing prayer. But that would make us sound like experts.

When it comes to our youth groups, we're the experts. But when it comes to your ministry, *you're* the expert. You're the one who knows your teens, your church, your families, your adult volunteers, your community, and your budget. So as much as we wish we could just hand you a ministry plan, we can't. And we shouldn't. A truly missional youth ministry can only grow out of the unique gifts and needs of the young people in your group.

So instead of a plan, we've created a series of questions to guide you as you develop a missional youth ministry. As you plan your next lock-in, Bible study, retreat, or fellowship event, let these questions shape your dreaming and planning. They can help you find ways to imbed a sense of mission into everything you do, build deeper relationships, involve others in the planning process, utilize volunteers, attend to various learning styles, and allow space for worship and prayer.

Mission

If mission is about taking part in God's work in the world, consider how each activity will help your teens learn more about that work or be an active part of it.

- How can you use this event to connect young people with missional themes such as justice, peace, and love?
- How will you develop the activity so that young people focus on the needs of others and not just their own?
- In what ways can you promote a healthy sense of mission-related risk in this event?
- Are there ways you can tie this activity to a local mission concern?
- Are there ways you can connect this activity with a global mission concern?
- How can you practice the missional theme of radical inclusion as you invite participation in this event or activity?
- Could you move this event out of the church and into a public area where outsiders might be invited to participate?

Relationship Building

Whether you're planning a game night or a weekend retreat, think about how you'll help the participants build stronger relationships.

- How will you help participants learn each other's names?
- What approaches will you use to welcome visitors and new members?
- How will you balance your activities to meet the needs of both introverts and extroverts?
- Which parts of the event will be intentionally set aside for young people to learn and share about themselves?
- Are there ways to transform possible competitive activities into cooperative team-building experiences?

- What opportunities will there be for teenagers to get to know each other better?
- How will you provide time for youth and adults to hang out?
- How will you provide time for you to connect with the youth?
- How can you create space for participants to deepen their relationships with Christ?

Planning

Consider how you'll intentionally develop the activity or program.

- What are you planning for—program, entertainment, or ministry?
- How will this event or experience connect with your ministry's long-range missional goals?
- How will you ground your planning in prayer?
- Are you willing to try new approaches, such as getting rid of the curriculum?
- What will you do if you plan for 20 people and only two show up, or vice versa?
- How will you feel if your plan doesn't go the way you wanted?
- Is there any way you could team with other churches or groups?
- How are you involving teenagers in the planning?
- How are you involving other adults in the planning?
- What other groups or people in the church need to be informed of your plans?

Spiritual Mentors

Think about how you'll use the gifts and talents of other adult leaders.

- How can you intentionally include intergenerational adult leadership in this activity?
- How will you tap the gifts of your mentors for this activity?
- In what ways can your spiritual mentors help lead the activity?
- Are there other adult mentors in the church who might be particularly gifted for this activity?

- How will you create an environment that allows mentors to provide spiritual leadership and guidance?
- What will you do if the mentors' approach or ideas during the event don't match your own?
- How might you include the participation of parents in this activity?
- How will you help volunteers reflect on this experience afterward?

Teaching and Learning

Every activity in youth ministry involves learning of some kind, whether it's a Bible study or a volleyball game. Consider the educational implications of your activity.

- How will you attend to the needs of the visual learners in the group?
- How will you attend to the needs of the auditory learners in the group?
- How will you attend to the needs of the tactile learners in the group?
- In what ways can you be intentional about connecting new learning to old learning?
- How will you help young people make an emotional connection with the subject?
- What experiences can you incorporate into the activity that will undergird your content?
- What opportunities will you provide for reflection throughout the learning process?
- How will you build in break time for your teens' brains to rest?
- What will you use as a *hook* for learning the content?
- How will you evaluate the success of your teaching efforts?

Worship and Prayer

Part of being a community of faith is worshipping together. Think about how worship will be integrated into your plans.

- In what ways will worship be tied to the theme of your activity?
- What worship experiences can you include that are relational?
- How can you develop a worship time that's experiential?

- What worship experiences can you include to inspire a sense of awe?
- How will you design the worship experiences to help youth see the world in a new way?
- Are there ways to create a new worship setting that fits with your event theme or focus?
- How will you attend to the various multiple intelligences during the worship time?
- What opportunities will there be for silence?
- What opportunities will there be for young people to share their individual joys and concerns?
- How will you ground the worship experience so it relates to the everyday experiences of your teenagers?

In the Gospel of Matthew, Jesus issues a challenge not only to those early followers of the Way, but to us as well: "Go therefore and make disciples of all nations, baptizing them in the name of the Father and of the Son and of the Holy Spirit, and teaching them to obey everything that I have commanded you" (Matthew 28:19-20 NRSV). Youth ministry has a number of essential elements—relationships, worship, fellowship, and education. But in the end, it's really about just one thing: Jesus' call to take part in the mission of joining in and leading others to follow a life of peace, love, justice, and saving grace that leads right to the heart of God.

When we dare to think about youth ministry holistically and to incorporate the spirit of the Way of Christ into everything we do—from lock-ins to mission trips, from game nights to campfire worship—we're inviting young people to experience a missional way of life in which God's Spirit is evident in all they say and do. Perhaps the greatest blessing that any of us who work with teens can experience is to watch missional youth become missional adults—those who understand God's call as a way of life centered on inviting others into the alternative reality of God's kingdom.

Share Your Thoughts

With the Author: Your comments will be forwarded to the author when you send them to *zauthor@zondervan.com*.

With Zondervan: Submit your review of this book by writing to *zreview@zondervan.com*.

Free Online Resources at

www.zondervan.com

Zondervan AuthorTracker: Be notified whenever your favorite authors publish new books, go on tour, or post an update about what's happening in their lives at www.zondervan.com/authortracker.

Daily Bible Verses and Devotions: Enrich your life with daily Bible verses or devotions that help you start every morning focused on God. Visit www.zondervan.com/newsletters.

Free Email Publications: Sign up for newsletters on Christian living, academic resources, church ministry, fiction, children's resources, and more. Visit www.zondervan.com/newsletters.

Zondervan Bible Search: Find and compare Bible passages in a variety of translations at www.zondervanbiblesearch.com.

Other Benefits: Register yourself to receive online benefits like coupons and special offers, or to participate in research.

ZONDERVAN.com/
AUTHORTRACKER
follow your favorite authors